IMAGES OF WAR

THE FRENCH ARMY ON THE SOMME 1916

Calf deep in mud, a signaller struggles to lay a line down a waterlogged trench, 3 November 1916. Drainage was hampered by the clay subsoil prevalent across the region, and even a summer shower could produce a morass. 'The Somme was mud!' cried Léon Guichard, who served with a colonial regiment. 'Mud! It was mud, just mud! The dead, even the wounded, used to fall into the communication trenches where they were trampled underfoot. It was mud! Mud! Mud! This was in the month of September: September, October, November . . . The relief came on 18 November 1916.'

IMAGES OF WAR

THE FRENCH ARMY ON THE SOMME 1916

RARE PHOTOGRAPHS FROM WARTIME ARCHIVES

Ian Sumner

Pen & Sword
MILITARY

First published in Great Britain in 2018 by
PEN & SWORD MILITARY
an imprint of
Pen & Sword Books Ltd,
47 Church Street,
Barnsley,
South Yorkshire
S70 2AS

Every effort has been made to trace the copyright of all the photographs.
If there are unintentional omissions, please contact the publisher in writing, who will
correct all subsequent editions.

ISBN 978 1 52672 548 6

The right of Ian Sumner to be identified as Author of this Work has been asserted
by him in accordance with the Copyright, Designs and Patents Act 1988.

A CIP record for this book is available from the British Library.

Typeset by CHIC GRAPHICS

Printed and bound by CPI Group (UK) Ltd, Croydon, CR0 4YY

Pen & Sword Aviation, Pen & Sword Family History, Pen & Sword Maritime, Pen &
Sword Military, Pen & Sword Discovery, Wharncliffe Local History, Wharncliffe True
Crime, Wharncliffe Transport, Pen and Sword Select, Pen and Sword Military Classics,
Leo Cooper, The Praetorian Press, Remember When, Seaforth Publishing and
Frontline Publishing.

For a complete list of Pen & Sword titles please contact
Pen & Sword Books Limited
47 Church Street, Barnsley, South Yorkshire, S70 2AS, England
E-mail: enquiries@pen-and-sword.co.uk
Website: www.pen-and-sword.co.uk

Contents

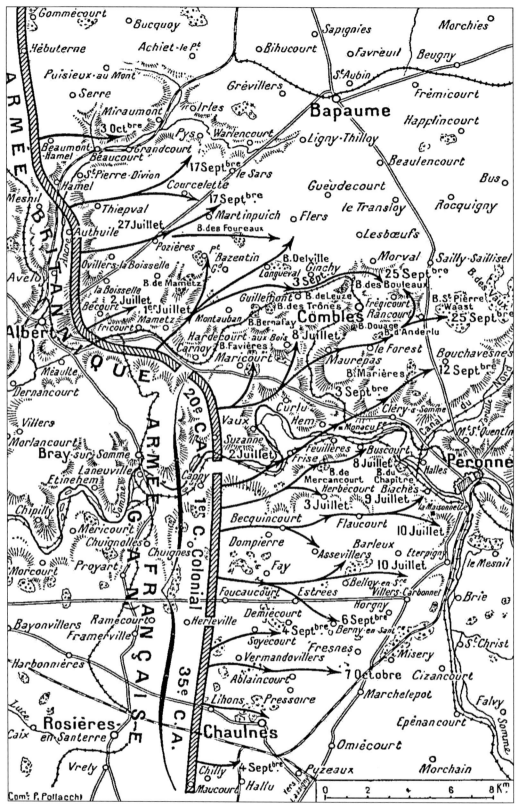

The battle of the Somme, showing the opening positions of the French and British forces on 1 July 1916, and the gains made during the offensive.

Introduction and Acknowledgements

Close to the open northern border of France, the Somme valley and its surrounding chalk downlands have long been a battleground.

In the course of their passage, with fire and steel, the enemy surpassed themselves in cruelty, inhumanity and barbarity. They rampaged through Picardy, destroying everything in their path. . . Not satisfied with killing men, they tore them to pieces . . . they abused women, bashed infants against walls . . . After they withdrew . . . dead bodies, bones and animal carcasses littered the ground all over upper Picardy.

These words date not from 1916, nor 1914, nor even the Franco-German war of 1870–1, when battles were fought at Pont-Noyelles, Bapaume and Saint-Quentin. Instead they were written in 1636, during the Thirty Years War, and the invaders were not German but Spanish – halted on the river Somme, at Corbie, just east of Amiens.

With its multiple branches, few crossings and, from 1843 onwards, an adjoining canal, the Somme presented a formidable obstacle to invaders. Rising north-east of the fortress town of Saint-Quentin, the river changes direction several times as it meanders through the *département* that bears its name. In the area of the 1916 battlefield, it first flows north-westwards between the fortress towns of Ham and Péronne, then turns west, describing great horseshoe loops as far as the regional capital, Amiens, where it finally swings north-west once more en route to the sea. The Somme and its tributaries – principally the Ancre to the north, and the Avre to the south – cut steep-sided valleys some 50m deep, separating areas of open plateau covered by a layer of loam over impermeable clay that turns quickly to mud, even in a heavy summer shower. Meanwhile the valley bottoms are broad and marshy, dotted with many small streams – permanent and seasonal.

The Franco-British offensive launched here on 1 July 1916 was planned as the major operation on the Western Front that year, part of a wider scheme of orchestrated Allied offensives that also encompassed Russia, Italy and the Balkans. For Britain, the Somme has acquired mythic status, its huge sacrifice of life for limited, hard-won gains coming to symbolize the First World War. For France, in contrast, the focus of remembrance is the contemporaneous struggle to halt the Germans at Verdun, an epic of endurance that cost the nation a million men – dead, missing and wounded. The role of French forces on the Somme, and their considerable success in the early weeks of the battle, has thus been largely eclipsed: with few exceptions, Anglophone writers cast the battle in purely British terms; their French counterparts focus on Verdun.

This book aims to help address this lacuna, illuminate a neglected aspect of the battle and give due recognition to the contribution made by French troops. I extend my thanks to all who have helped in its writing, particularly my wife Margaret, for her translating and editing skills, but also the staffs of the Service Historique de la Défense at Vincennes, the Bibliothèque Nationale in Paris, the municipal libraries of Albi, Dijon, Meaux and Tours, and the British Library. Like my previous titles in the Images of War series, the photographs used are drawn from the exceptionally rich French official archive held by the Bibliothèque de Documentation Internationale et Contemporaine, Université de Paris-Nanterre. My thanks go to them and the following named photographers:

Allard: frontispiece, 66 (bottom), 108 (top), 128 (top), 130 (top)
de Boissières: 19
Branger: 31
de Camondo: 53 (top), 116 (top), 138 (top)
Canet de Chizy: 73 (bottom)
Chénau: 16 (top)
Frèrejouan du Saint: 143 (top)
Gallier: 14 (top), 62 (top)
Guérdan: 142 (bottom)
Lapido: 21 (bottom)
Malicet: 13 (bottom)
Malroux: 22 (top), 23 (top)

Moreau: 30 (bottom), 34 (bottom), 35 (top)
Muraz: 134
Olivetti: 21 (top), 25 (both), 28 (bottom), 33 (top), 36
Peyval: 65 (top), 104 (top), 123 (top)
Pompée: 15, 20 (top), 28, 29 (top), 33 (bottom)
de Preissac: 37 (both)
Reussner: 59 (top), 60 (bottom), 65 (bottom), 72 (bottom)
Roumens: 82
Rouyer: 52 (top)
Simon: 16 (bottom), 30 (top)

Note: Unless otherwise stated, all dates are 1916 and all places lie in the *département* of the Somme. Some locations came at different times under French and under British control. These are: Bois d'Anderlu = Anderlu Wood; Bois de Bernafay = Bernafay Wood; Ferme de Bronfay = Bronfay Farm; Bois des Loges = Lodge Wood; Ferme de Monacu = Monacu Farm; Ferme de Toutvent (now Touvent) = Toutvent Farm; Bois de Trônes = Trônes Wood; Bois Y = Y Wood.

Further Reading

Les Armées françaises dans la Grande Guerre, Tome IV, volumes 2 and 3, with
   associated volumes of annexes and maps (Paris: Imprimerie Nationale, 1933)
Doughty, Robert. *Pyrrhic Victory: French Strategy and Operations in the Great War*
   (Cambridge, MA: Belknap, 2008)
O'Mara, David. *The Somme 1916: Touring the French Sector* (Barnsley: Pen & Sword,
   2018)
Philpott, William. *Bloody Victory: The Sacrifice on the Somme* (London: Little, Brown,
   2009)
Strohn, Matthias (ed.). *The Battle of the Somme* (London: Osprey, 2016)

Chapter One

1914-1915

On the outbreak of war in August 1914, the Germans marched swiftly through neutral Belgium, before turning south to invade France. On the Somme, the French were driven back on both sides of the river: to the north, around Moislains, on 28 August; to the south, near Proyart, the following day. The fortress town of Péronne fell on the 28th, and the regional capital, Amiens, three days later, but within a week the German advance was halted by a Franco-British force at the battle of the Marne. The enemy withdrew, allowing French troops to re-enter Amiens, but south-east of the Somme, on the river Aisne, the Germans managed to check Allied progress. Both sides then swung north again, each probing for a weakness, trying to turn their opponent's flank in the series of leapfrogging movements subsequently named the 'Race to the Sea'.

In late September, the two forces clashed again on the Somme in a second series of meeting engagements. South of the river, Allies and Germans fought each other to a standstill on the open Santerre plateau, between Chaulnes and Péronne, before switching the point of attack to the north bank, each vainly seeking the enemy's open flank. With poor intelligence failing to pinpoint the exact position of the Germans, the French suffered a number of setbacks, every attempted advance provoking determined resistance and counter-attacks. On 29 September they captured but could not hold the village of Fricourt, 5km east of Albert, while successfully fighting off a German counter-attack designed to seize the town itself.

As the battle moved north towards Arras (Pas-de-Calais) and Ypres (West-Vlaanderen), neither side was able to win the upper hand, and to consolidate their gains the opposing troops began to dig in where they were. The next month brought a host of minor actions as the two forces struggled to seize small advantages of ground, but mutual exhaustion and shortages of ammunition quickly produced a stalemate. In mid-December, General Joseph Joffre, the French commander-in-chief, tried to break the deadlock by ordering an attack all along the front line, but bad weather and woefully inadequate artillery support doomed his initiative to failure. North of the Somme, around Mametz and Maricourt, on 17–18 December, the regiments of 53rd Division lost over 3,000 men yet scarcely breached the German wire; while 5km north-west, around Ovillers (now Ovillers-la-Boisselle), the Bretons of 19th Infantry suffered 1,150 casualties with no greater success.

In 1915 and early 1916 the French sought to force a breakthrough by launching bloody and fruitless offensives in Champagne and, with British support, in Artois. The Somme, meanwhile, was considered a 'quiet' sector, as no large-scale operations took place here. Quiet, however, was a relative term. Scarred by their failed attempts to cross no man's land, French and Germans alike were driven underground, seeking to dig tunnels beneath the opposing front line, explode a huge charge and exploit the opportunities thus created to seize sections of the enemy trenches. To counter the danger, both sides dug yet more tunnels, hoping to intercept the enemy and explode smaller charges (*camouflets*) to destroy his work. The Somme valley was too marshy for such operations, but the surrounding soft chalk downland provided ideal terrain. During the spring and early summer of 1915, mine and counter-mine were dug and exploded, followed by hand-to-hand fighting for control of the resulting craters: at La Boisselle, north of the river, seven main charges were set off by the two sides; south of the river, eleven French and twenty-one German mines were detonated at Beuvraignes, as well as sixty-seven French and thirty-four German mines and *camouflets* at Fay.

The only set-piece action took place on 7 June 1915, when the French Second Army mounted a diversionary attack in the far north of the sector, supporting the main Allied offensive in neighbouring Artois. Attacking across open, virtually flat terrain, the Second Army's objective was to take the enemy trenches around Ferme de Toutvent, between the villages of Hébuterne and Serre. Despite heavy casualties the French achieved a tactical success, with the farm captured and held in the face of fierce German counter-attacks from 10 to 13 June; yet strategically the attack was a failure, lacking the overall strength to pull in the enemy reserves. Meanwhile every regiment involved suffered enormously: 64th Infantry, for example, lost 1,100 men during a week in the trenches at Hébuterne. Such was the scale of French losses – incurred here and in the main offensives in Champagne and Artois – that Joffre was compelled to take action. His allies were pressed to assume responsibility for more of the front line, and in August the newly created British Third Army moved into place, taking control of a 26km sector running south from Hébuterne as far as the Somme at the village of Curlu.

Marching infantry fall out for a break, September 1914. In the background, Algerian Tirailleurs press on. Mobilized in August in Nancy (Meurthe-et-Moselle), the men of 26th Infantry (XX Corps) had already seen action several times in Lorraine before a combination of trains and old-fashioned marching brought them to the Somme in late September. 'The whole region was on fire,' they discovered. 'Albert, Fricourt, Mametz were in flames.'

The Germans march into shell-damaged Péronne, 29 August 1914. Writing under the pseudonym 'Fasol', local journalist Henri Douchet noted how quickly the enemy seized control: 'the German occupation is reaching further and further across town, much to the annoyance of those premises, more numerous every day, grabbed by the Kommandatur'. By November Douchet was reporting that 'all weapons and munitions in local hands must be deposited in front of the town hall ... Anyone subsequently found with a weapon will be shot. Should any hostile acts [be committed], and particularly shots fired, while German troops are in residence, the town will be put to the torch.'

Both French and Germans created ad hoc regimental cemeteries during the 'Race to the Sea'. Erected near Dompierre, this grave marker commemorates men of I Bavarian Corps: 'Here Bavarian heroes rest in peace, fell 1914'. The *département* of the Somme now houses eleven German military cemeteries: the largest, at Vermandovillers, remembers 22,632 men; Fricourt, 17,031; and Rancourt, 11,422.

The Albert–Bapaume road passes through the village of Pozières, prior to the war. Positioned on a breezy ridge above the river Ancre, this community of some 300 souls was the highest point of the Somme battlefield and thus a vital Allied objective. It would be well fortified by the Germans and eventually captured by 1st Australian Division in late July 1916, only after bitter, bloody fighting. Nothing remained of the village: 'The whole area was flayed and pounded into a veritable sea of shell-craters,' reported the Australian war correspondent, and later official historian, Charles Bean.

Many civilians were driven from their homes, but others chose to stay put. In 1915, this group is braving the enemy bombardment in Frise, a riverside village on the south bank of the Somme, almost within the front lines. 'The bell tower at Frise was brought down by Boche shellfire,' reported Blaise Cendrars (3rd Régiment de Marche, 1st Régiment Étranger). 'No fewer than 122 shells were used. The church was doomed anyway, as the village was destroyed by German incendiaries.' French troops clung on here until 28 January 1916, when they were forced out by a local attack. By July 1916, 3,580 refugees from front-line villages were seeking sanctuary in Amiens. Thereafter numbers soared, with 27,900 sheltering in Avesnes (Pas-de-Calais) and district by October 1916.

Men of 79th Infantry are busy maintaining their rifles and equipment, Gommecourt (Pas-de-Calais), October 1914. Crude and narrow by later standards, the front-line trenches here in the far north of the later Somme battlefield were named after streets in the regiment's home town of Nancy (Meurthe-et-Moselle): Rue Clodion and Rue de la Paix, for example.

Men of 10th Company, 104th Infantry occupy a recently dug position, Tilloloy/Beuvraignes, November 1914. Now bisected by the A1 motorway and a high-speed TGV rail line, the village of Tilloloy remained firmly in French hands throughout the war, while neighbouring Beuvraignes (2km to the east) lay behind German lines. After three weeks of bitter combat, in late October the front lines stablized here, just metres apart, on the western outskirts of Beuvraignes. Nearest the camera is Captain Marius-Albert Peltier, CO of 10th Company, who would be killed at Perthes (Marne) during the Champagne offensive in 1915. His men had received orders to dig in where they stood – just one small contribution to the continuous lines of trenches that soon extended from the North Sea to the Swiss border. The trench remains a crude affair and, with no official provision yet made for cold-weather clothing, the men are clad in a variety of scarves and balaclavas, most likely sent from home.

Resting on a pile of logs, a soldier of 22nd Infantry scribbles a letter from reserve positions near Méricourt-sur-Somme, March 1915. Withdrawn from the Vosges front in September 1914, the regiment transferred by train to Picardy and was thrown into action south of the river around Fay and Foucaucourt-en-Santerre. In April 1915 came a move to nearby Fontaine-lès-Cappy: 'What happened to our wonderful Foucaucourt trenches!' they lamented. '[Now] we're positioned just a few metres from the Germans in a line of huge craters created by the explosion of powerful mines, in collapsed communications trenches, with no front-line trenches nor barbed wire.'

A working party returns wearily to its billet, Lihons, March 1915. The village lay south of the river, some 200m behind the front lines, with reserve trenches running through its lanes and gardens. At nearby Chuignes in May 1916, Charles Barberon (121st Heavy Artillery) noted that the 1914 harvest had not been brought home: 'The [crops] flowered in 1915, and their long dry stems poke from the surrounding grasses. Here's a field of lucerne, virtually untouched. But usually nothing recognizable is left. Wild flowers have smothered it all. Here are swathes of poppies, fields full of mustard, great masses of thistles, cornflowers, sorrel, nettles. It's the very image of the war, civilisation retreating before the barbarian hordes.'

Still in his pre-war uniform, dragoons officer Lieutenant Lescot uses a periscope to survey the German lines, near Albert, June 1915. The trench wall has been converted into a ramp to provide a quick exit in case of an assault. Cavalry divisions were often positioned behind the front lines to exploit any breakthrough; by mid-1915, however, most cavalry regiments had created a 'light group' that performed dismounted tours of duty in the trenches, particularly in quieter sectors. Historian Augustin Cochin (146th Infantry) would be killed in front of Hardécourt-aux-Bois on 8 July: 'It's said that the cavalry won't survive this present conflict; but nor will the infantry (no morbid pun intended). All that will remain will be gunners and pioneers, craters and shells.'

Men in the front-line trenches wear the new-pattern camouflage greatcoat, near Frise, 1915. The greatcoats varied considerably in their detail – pockets, buttons, etc. – and, to economize on cloth, single-breasted patterns were soon preferred. The collar-patches seen here display the regimental number on a yellow background, but these were quickly deemed too conspicuous and replaced by patches in the same horizon blue (a light bluish-grey) as the coat. These men are still wearing the traditional kepi and *bonnet de police*: the distribution of steel Adrian helmets would not begin until the autumn. 'We've just had a lot of kit handed out,' enthused Robert Fernier (15th Chasseurs). 'Now none of us look as if we've just come out of the trenches: the monk is made by his habit, and civilians will no longer need feel ashamed on our behalf.'

A soldier peers through a loophole towards the German positions, L'Échelle-Saint-Aurin, September 1915. The village lay on the banks of the Avre, just north of Tilloloy. With the evening light behind him, this man risks appearing in silhouette to any enemy sniper. In the background, two men have just brought up the rations, carried in pails suspended from a shoulder yoke.

Men of 22nd Territorials guard a well-constructed front-line position, near Authuille, 1915. The village of Authuille lay in the Ancre valley, just below the Thiepval ridge, in a sector taken over by the British on 31 July 1915. The gunner wears the kepi and horizon-blue greatcoat, his sleeve bearing his skill-at-arms badge – the crossed guns of a machine-gunner. His trousers remain the dark-blue corduroy provisional pattern issued the previous winter. The gun is the weighty but reliable 1914 Hotchkiss, whose ammunition was contained in 24-round aluminium trays. It could fire between 400 and 600 rounds a minute, with a range of 1800m.

A sentry with a sniperscope keeps an eye on the Germans opposite, Tilloloy/Beuvraignes, September 1915. Meanwhile his comrades read the papers: *Le Matin* was a populist title of the right; *Le Journal* offered a more centrist and literary perspective but still enjoyed a circulation of one million. The two sides detonated thirty-two mines under the front lines here during 1915. To the rear, however, the village of Tilloloy 'was a decent spot', according to Blaise Cendrars (3rd Régiment de Marche, 1st Régiment Étranger). 'Except for the howitzers firing on Beuvraignes at noon, nothing ever happened there.'

A sentry is well swaddled against the weather, Côte 97, just south of Tilloloy, winter 1915. 'On guard duty in the front line, whatever the sector, you never had any shelter from rain, snow, hail or other foul weather,' recalled Édouard Legros (295th Infantry). 'You had to stand on the spot for two hours, with no means of escape. Sometimes icicles would be dangling from your moustache.' His tent section, 'a rag', proved useless. In the end, however, he found the answer in a scrounged British goatskin and rubberized groundsheet.

This crude, uncomfortably shallow trench, 'La Barricade', lay just 5–20m from enemy lines, Tilloloy/Beuvraignes, December 1915. No man's land in this sector was pockmarked with numerous craters created by the mine explosions, while to the south-east, the poste de la Croix lay in a dangerous salient, on a downslope exposed to fire on three sides. 'No cross or calvary had ever stood in this accursed spot, which more closely resembled the cauldrons of hell,' recalled Blaise Cendrars. 'No man wanted to go forward to the Croix.'

A battery of Cellerier mortars is positioned in the trenches, Tilloloy/Beuvraignes. The Cellerier was a crude 65mm tube fixed to a block of wood and fired by a charge of gunpowder. Easy to construct, it was first introduced as a makeshift in November 1914, but examples remained in service until 1917.

This front-line dugout contains a 60mm Brandt pneumatic mortar, Tilloloy, September 1915. Introduced as a potential replacement for the Cellerier, the Brandt fired a bomb with fins that deployed in flight, as demonstrated by the man seated (left rear). Tanks filled with compressed air provided the power, and a supplementary air reservoir could be filled using a foot pump. At a rate of ten, very accurate, rounds a minute, the mortar had a range of c.230m, and some 500 examples were brought into service, but they proved very difficult to maintain and were phased out in favour of the British Stokes.

Men of 22nd Territorials tend their mobile cooker, Aveluy, 1915. The village of Aveluy lay 2km south of Authuille in the Ancre valley, in the sector later transferred to British control. The French introduced mobile cookers from 1915, relieving each infantry section of the need to cater for itself. Cooks were given an official cookery manual, compiled by restaurateur Prosper Montagné, featuring plenty of recipes for stews and soups. Montagné was aware that army cooks 'have innumerable difficulties to overcome to serve their comrades with food as good as conditions will allow'. But not every soldier was quite so sympathetic. 'You can imagine what the stew's like,' grumbled one disgruntled soldier. 'It's always cold because some poor fellows have had to carry it for three or four kilometres.'

The food has arrived in the trenches held by men of 22nd Territorials, near Authuille, 1915. Although often of poor quality and indifferently prepared, the regular supply of bread and meat represented a notable improvement in diet for many men from poor rural backgrounds, where meat was a rarity and bread baked only once every three or four weeks.

With local farms evacuated, soldiers harvest apples and load them into a cider press, Tilloloy, September 1915. Each man was allowed a daily wine ration – 37.5cl in 1914, increased to 50cl in 1917. But wine was not the drink of choice in every part of France: men from Normandy, Brittany and Maine drank cider, and regiments could substitute 100cl of cider where local circumstances allowed.

The NCOs of 16th Territorials enjoy a convivial gathering in their mess, Arvillers, March 1916. The village of Arvillers lay south of the river, on the Santerre plateau. After time in the trenches in Flanders, the regiment was now employed providing working parties for the heavy artillery. Its pre-war depot was in Péronne, so these men were no doubt glad to be back on home soil, even if some now lay behind enemy lines.

A captain relaxes in his dugout, Bois des Loges, January 1916. The walls are decorated with pin-ups snipped from the pages of *La Vie Parisienne*. 'Of all the illustrated magazines, *La Vie Parisienne* – with its Gerda Wegener prints of a tiny female in corset and bloomers – is certainly the most popular,' reckoned Captain Charles Delvert (101st Infantry). 'I find it every time time I visit an HQ. Minnies and heavy shells are falling even now . . . but to my right a voluptuous, saucer-eyed blonde languorously draped over an armchair reminds me that elsewhere life goes on; that incarceration and death are reserved only for the poilu; that 200 kilometres away people are enjoying all the pleasures of civilization.'

A long 120mm cannon is in position, near Cappy, 1915. Its trail is dug in to give extra elevation over the ridge off right. Plates – *cingoli* – are fitted to the wheels to stop them sinking into the soft ground. In the background lie the Somme and the village of Cappy: '[It] lay in a depression behind a rise of ground about a kilometer and a half from the line,' recalled American volunteer ambulance driver Robert Whitney Imbrie (SSU1). 'In peace times it was doubtless a rather attractive little place of perhaps three hundred people. Now, devastated by days and months of bombardment, and the passing of countless soldiers, deserted by its civil population and invaded by countless rats, it presented an aspect forlorn beyond imagination. On a gray winter's day, with sleet beating down and deepening the already miry roads, and a dreary wind whistling through the shattered houses, the place cried out with the desolation of war.'

These men have improvised an artillery observation post on top of a haystack, near Cappy, 1915. The extra elevation gives them a view eastwards over the German lines on the Flaucourt plateau, towards Péronne. The pre-war army had devoted little attention to heavy artillery or indirect fire, so the trench stalemate forced troops to adopt expedients of this kind.

Two officers demonstrate different methods of firing signals, near Authuille, 1915. The three variants comprise (left to right) a flare pistol, an obsolete Gras rifle modified to fire flares, and a rocket. The guns were often required to fire on targets out of direct line of sight, so communication between the men in the trenches and their supporting artillery was vital. As telephone lines were highly vulnerable to shell-fire, visual signals such as flares and rockets in pre-arranged colours were also used.

A wounded man is evacuated from Ambulance 6/4, Château de Warsy, November 1914. The vehicle has been commandeered from a wine wholesaler, but the number of smiling soldiers suggests this is only a drill. The 6/4 (i.e. the 6th Field Ambulance Unit of IV Corps) was scattered around this village in the Avre valley – in the château, the church and a nearby barn. This arrangement, lamented the war diary, along with 'sluggish bureaucratic procedures', led to delays in treating the wounded.

An armoured 220 locomotive, probably from the Paris-Lyon-Méditerranée (PLM) company, hauls a rake of unarmoured carriages, Ribemont-Méricourt station, January 1915. Armoured protection was used for rolling stock operating near the front lines, as here in the Ancre valley, between Amiens and Albert. True armoured trains, with carriages armoured as well, usually mounted artillery of various calibres.

The famous Leaning Virgin of Albert has been hit by enemy shells, March 1915. The tower, with its gilded statue of the Virgin Mary, crowned the Basilica of Our Lady of Brebières, completed in 1897. The Germans believed the tower contained a French artillery observation post, only 3km from the front lines, and from October 1914 shelled it accordingly. On 7 January 1915 the dome was destroyed; a fortnight later, the base of the statue was hit, causing the Virgin to tilt alarmingly. According to popular legend, the war would end when the Virgin fell. The tower was finally demolished by British artillery in 1918.

Rings made from shell caps were much-prized souvenirs. 'A lot of these men are peasants or labourers accustomed to manual work, so how do they keep busy, pass the time and drive away "the blues"?' observed Lieutenant Émile Morin (60th Infantry). 'They use battlefield debris: flare- or shell-cases; brass or aluminium rockets; the driving bands from shell caps; cartridges and bullets.' Here, a crowd of potential customers – including a man holding a shell-case – watch as a craftsman sets to work, Tilloloy, December 1915. 'I'm glad you got your rings all right,' one soldier had written home that July. 'They'll make a nice little keepsake, made at the front.'

Men of a divisional stretcher-bearer unit relax to the strains of a violin, Authuille, 1915. One lucky unit included virtuoso Lucien Durosoir (1878–1955). In February 1916, after a melancholy day burying the dead, the CO approached him: 'So, Durosoir, shall we have a few tunes again soon?' With the greatest of pleasure, replied the musician. But fate soon intervened: 'The house I occupied in Cappy was flattened by a shell, burying my violin and Dumant's too. It was only three weeks since he'd had it sent.'

Théodore Botrel (1868–1925) performs before a crowd of soldiers, Cappy, 1915. Poet, playwright, singer and prolific composer of patriotic songs, Botrel was much lauded in certain sections of the press. Yet he and his songs were by no means universally popular: 'Everyone ordered on "Botrel fatigues" did anything they could to get out of them,' claimed Lieutenant Émile Morin (60th Infantry).

The village of La Boisselle is viewed from a point in the French lines later named Usna Hill by the British, winter 1915. The French were occupying the left side of the village, in ruins; the German positions lay to the right. In the centre is the village cemetery. The Albert–Bapaume road crosses the photograph, while Mash Valley is off to the left.

A mine crater is put into a state of defence, La Boisselle, 1915. Plentiful boxes for hand grenades have been set in the lip of the trench. The French and Germans alike had exploded a number of mines under a farmyard at the south-western edge of the village, producing a crater field known to the French as the Îlot, to the Germans as the Granatenhof, and to its later British occupants as the Glory Hole.

Protected under a mound of sandbags is the entrance to a mine, La Boisselle, winter 1915. 118th Infantry undertook a tour of duty here between November 1914 and August 1915: 'Then began the real trench and mining war. The houses became citadels, turned by both sides into strongpoints. Face to face, it would be an unrelenting, mortal struggle, harrowing from the constant vigilance imposed upon the sentries, the dread of mines and minnies. The Îlot formed by the conquered houses was held due solely to the magnificent coolness, tenacity and endurance of our men.'

German prisoners are marched through the streets of Mailly-Maillet, 7 June 1915. They had been captured in the fighting around Ferme de Toutvent, near Hébuterne. Charles Barberon (121st Heavy Artillery) saw the German troops as fellow sufferers: 'A lot of French soldiers watch the prisoners go by,' he wrote the following year. 'I never hear a bad word. Their attitude is quite different to that of the civilians I saw last year in Sainte-Ménehould. Surprisingly, the soldier under fire does not share the civilians' hatred of the enemy.'

French soldiers of 22nd Territorials visit a battalion of Argyll and Sutherland Highlanders, near Authuille, 1915. The British took over this sector on 31 July 1915, when 22nd Territorials were relieved by 2/5th Lancashire Fusiliers. James Racine (1/5th Seaforth Highlanders) was a near neighbour: 'Here we found large dugouts and the French troops had evidently believed in comfort, for they had constructed beds, made from struts and covered with wire netting, which were very comfortable. They had also constructed rustic tables and chairs. In an old house I found a very much out of tune piano and accompanied a mixture of French and British troops in a singsong. The French troops gave us a hearty welcome and informed us that the sector was extremely quiet and that only eight light shells a day were fired into the village. They were sent over in pairs at the following times 11am, 2pm, 4pm, and 8pm, and the French artillery replied similarly. At the times stated, the trench troops had gone into the dugouts, whilst the shells burst, and returned to the estaminets at the conclusion of the comic bombardment.'

French liaison officers visit the British front-line trenches, Hébuterne. It was here on the Somme that Sylvain Wannemacher (109th Infantry) first encountered his allies: 'We've met our first British,' he reported. 'They're sharing their billets in the village with us. We admire the facilities and the way they've organized their comforts even in wartime. They've a place with a mess where they can pick up supplies: wine, beer, all kinds of drinks, cigarettes, canned food … I'm rushing off for some cigarettes but my pocket won't stretch far.'

Gommecourt Park, 1916. Pictured here from Hébuterne, this wooded park formed a heavily fortified salient jutting from the enemy lines into no man's land. The British 46th (North Midland) Division would attack the north side of the salient on 1 July 1916, only to be repulsed with heavy casualties.

Chapter Two

The Plans

General Joffre's plan for 1916 was to launch simultaneous offensives against the Central Powers on a number of fronts – in France, Russia, the Balkans and Italy. On 6 December 1915, at a conference of the Entente Powers held at the Grand Quartier Général (GQG) at Chantilly, he laid out his vision – a coordinated Allied action, gradually wearing down the enemy before striking the decisive blow. The conference ended two days later, having agreed an outline programme, but two more months of discussion were needed to settle the final plans for a joint Franco-British attack on the Somme in June 1916. The location was appealing on several grounds: the French and British sectors met here, facilitating a joint initiative; the ground was untouched by previous offensives; and, given the enormous scale of French losses in 1915, Joffre wanted to force the British to undertake a greater share of the fighting.

On the French side, responsibility for detailed planning went to General Ferdinand Foch, commander of Northern Army Group. But with preparations still at an embryonic stage, the surprise German attack on Verdun in late February 1916 threw everything into disarray. The weight of the enemy assault pulled in many of the French troops originally earmarked for the Somme, the French reserves were consumed, and plans for the summer offensive were hastily reworked. Instead of a joint operation, the British would now lead the attack, supported by the French – with the immediate aim of relieving the pressure on Verdun.

Foch was initially an attack-minded general. His writings formed, if indirectly, the theoretical underpinning of the methods of *attaque à l'outrance* which dominated pre-war French military thinking, and which in 1914 produced only catastrophically heavy casualties. During the battle of the Marne, Foch's own command, XX Corps, was among the formations that suffered huge losses in stemming the German advance, and as commander of Northern Army Group during the Artois offensives of 1915, the general came to modify his views. The breakthrough would 'probably not be effected in a single blow, but through repeated and sustained efforts', while charging the enemy wire with little or no artillery preparation, hoping to catch the Germans by surprise, was a recipe for disaster. In 1914, the artillery had played a supporting role, firing at close range while the infantry pressed home its attack at bayonet point, but for Foch this would no longer suffice. The artillery, 'the only [arm] capable of destroying enemy units', would now take primary responsibility for the attack, the infantry simply occupying enemy positions previously devastated by friendly fire. 'Experience has shown', Foch concluded, 'that wherever the artillery performs its task effectively, the infantry progresses easily and at minimal cost in men.'

So Foch foresaw a lengthy, methodical operation; one that would make much greater use of artillery firepower and continue until it had broken the German capacity to resist. The full weight of the barrage would fall on the German front line, believed to be the most heavily fortified; the second and subsequent lines of trenches were expected to be much weaker. The enemy batteries would be identified through extensive aerial reconnaissance, then subjected to counter-battery fire from the corps artillery:

> Our artillery must establish a clear ascendancy over the opposing guns before targeting the front-line trenches and entanglements. From then on, the barrage will be continuous. Unless completely neutralized before the infantry attacks, the enemy artillery will compromise the advance. Once initiated, the bombardment of the enemy artillery must be pursued continuously throughout the battle.

In his detailed instructions Foch outlined the role of artillery units at every level, ordered the creation of a transport and supply network, and described how the infantry should prepare and execute its attack. This would consist of successive assaults, carefully supported by a rolling artillery barrage, to continue for as long as proved necessary – a 'break-in' rather than a 'breakthrough' – a series of hammer-blows, designed to wear down the opposition until all resistance had evaporated. Infantry units must resist the temptation of making deep, unsupported advances into the German positions, which would only produce vulnerable salients:

> This must not be a simple assault conducted pell-mell towards its final objectives. A free-for-all always ends in confusion, i.e. chaos, units mixed up, control lost ... leaving commanders unable to issue orders, keep track of their men, or coordinate artillery and infantry actions to ensure artillery cover for the attacking troops.

Instead, mutually supporting infantry units would attack all along the line, supported by thorough but flexible artillery concentrations, advancing as far as the enemy artillery batteries, and leaving only the largest strongpoints to be subdued by the follow-up waves. Building on the approach successfully introduced by General Pétain at Verdun, regiments and brigades would also be rotated in and out of the line in quick succession to prevent exhaustion: 'it is vital to employ the infantry with strict economy, only demand efforts that are within its capabilities, and lead it firmly and methodically'.

As for aviation, Foch had once dismissed flying as mere sport; by 1916, however, he had come to recognize its potentially crucial role in battle. The 'essential role' of aircraft was to observe the enemy while denying French airspace to hostile reconnaissance missions, so air superiority was vital. After a provisional fighter unit had demonstrated its worth at Verdun, assembling the cream of French pilots first to seize, and then maintain, air superiority over the Meuse, denying French airspace to intruders and allowing friendly cooperation machines to operate unhindered across enemy lines, GQG now created the elite Groupement de Cachy, a provisional fighter unit based around squadron N3, the famous *Cigognes* (Storks). Finally, to provide continuity of surveillance and ensure the effective exploitation of its results, corps aviation commanders were to coordinate the work of their squadrons.

In planning his offensive, Foch originally demanded three armies: one army, six divisions strong, would sit astride the Somme, maintaining contact with the British and supporting the central army; the central army, sixteen divisions strong, would initially target the town of Roye, 30km south-west of Péronne, before turning north to push across the river and take Péronne from the rear; finally, a southern army, of eight divisions, would support the central army, while also capturing the fortress village of Lassigny (Oise). But with Verdun reducing the number of troops and guns available, Foch was forced to narrow the scope of his operation. The attacking front was reduced from 40km to 15km, and the number of French armies cut from three to one – Sixth Army (General Émile Fayolle) – with objectives now restricted to supporting the British immediately north of the Somme, and clearing all German artillery on the south bank of the river to protect the British flank and rear. Concerned at the shortage of resources, Foch suggested postponing the offensive until 1917, but Joffre and the politicians pressed to go ahead: the need to relieve Verdun was paramount.

At GQG, opinion was divided: 'Mount a really strong attack and the first shells will put an end to the assault on Verdun,' argued General Edmond Buat. 'Utter moonshine,' retorted General Édouard de Castelnau, the chief of staff. Yet Joffre remained an optimist, gradually withdrawing troops from other sectors to be deployed should Foch achieve a breakthrough.

In his final plan, Foch called for Sixth Army to attack straight ahead – its ultimate objective, the Bapaume–Péronne–Ham road, running north to south, behind and roughly parallel with the German front line. XX Corps (General Maurice Balfourier) would be positioned north of the Somme, supporting the British and advancing to the hills above Curlu. They faced a difficult task: their starting front of 2.6km would double by the time they reached the German third line, while successfully attaining their third objective, the Hem–Maurepas line, would depend on the British advance. South of the river, I Colonial Corps (General Pierre Berdoulat) would advance on a front of 1.2km to 1.5km to take the enemy positions between Frise and Dompierre, before pushing on another kilometre east to the German second position between the villages of Herbécourt and Assevillers. South again, XXXV Corps (General Charles Jacquot) was to establish a protective flank between the villages of Fay and Estrées, then push north-east to capture the open, rolling Flaucourt plateau, opposite Péronne, from where Jacquot could support the advance on the north bank of the Somme, while also denying the high ground to enemy artillery observers. Finally, II Corps (General Denis Duchêne) would remain in reserve. Diversions – sudden artillery concentrations, trench raids and gas attacks – would be launched to the south by Tenth Army (General Joseph Micheler), and if all went well, a further diversionary attack was envisaged around Beuvraignes, close to the neighbouring *département* of the Oise.

While speed would be vital in circumventing German resistance, the advance should not be reckless. It should 'proceed from objective to objective, maintaining the élan of the troops without leaving anything to chance', General Fayolle ordered his senior commanders. 'Each attack will have a defined objective of limited breadth and depth and be preceded by an artillery bombardment and a reconnaissance of the wire.' To support his attacks, Fayolle could count on 732 guns, including 122 heavy pieces, but he feared that the enhanced role of the artillery was starting to sap the infantry of its initiative. 'It's all down to the artillery', he commented.

> With pioneers in the van, territorials to the rear, artillery all around, the infantry will consent to stand guard in the trenches. But when the time comes to attack, they are unwilling to take any extra risks. Nothing can be done with them. If we attack, [they say] there are too many trenches. If the trenches have been flattened, they don't know where to go or where to fire.

The preliminary bombardment opened in fine weather on 24 June. But two days later it started to rain and, despite the newly laid narrow-gauge railway network, the gunners were struggling to replenish their shells. Some preliminary artillery objectives remained unmet, and the attack was postponed for two days until 1 July. Privately, Fayolle remained sceptical of the entire operation, especially of the need to tie French progress to the British advance:

Subordinate as we were to their offensive, we could do nothing but exploit a local success. Besides, this always was a meaningless battle. There was never any question of a breakthrough. And if a battle is not designed to produce a breakthrough, what purpose does it serve? Sixth Army was never going to find a way through on the banks of the Somme. All it could do was manoeuvre south [of the river].

General Sir Douglas Haig (1861–1928) inspects a guard of chasseurs à pied, Villa Poiret, Chantilly (Oise), 23 December 1915. Haig, the newly appointed commander of the British Expeditionary Force, has arrived to confer with General Joffre. Haig's predecessor, Sir John French, had already committed the BEF to coordinated attacks with the French, but here the topic of conversation was the possibility of an imminent German offensive. In Chantilly, GQG occupied the Hôtel du Grand Condé, a new six-storey building close to the station and the main Paris road, but for his private office Joffre had commandeered the Villa Poiret, preferring to work away from the hustle and bustle.

General Joseph Joffre (1852–1931) visits the headquarters of XXXV Corps, near Foucaucourt-en-Santerre, July 1916. His companion is General Paul Duparge (1849–1931), military secretary to the French president, Raymond Poincaré (1860–1934). After service in the Engineers, particularly in Africa and the Far East, Joffre was appointed as the army's chief of staff in 1911. On the outbreak of war, he assumed operational command of French forces at the front, becoming commander-in-chief of all French forces in the field on 2 December 1915. An organizer rather than a battlefield commander, he retained his faith in a decisive breakthrough battle long after subordinates like Foch had turned to a more considered, methodical approach.

General Ferdinand Foch (1851–1929), commander of Northern Army Group, bids farewell to General Joffre, Méricourt-sur-Somme. As an instructor at the French staff college, the artilleryman Foch had analysed Napoleonic warfare and identified the will to win as a key component of battlefield victory. His conclusions, however, were misapplied by advocates of the 'cult of the offensive' that swept through French military thought immediately before the war. To Foch, the will to win, though important to ultimate victory, was never its guarantee. Joffre believed the determined, combative Foch would work well with the British and make an ideal commander of the French contribution to the Allied offensive.

General Émile Fayolle (1852–1928), commander of Sixth Army, receives General Foch at Sixth Army headquarters, Méricourt-sur-Somme. On the verge of retirement when war broke out, the artilleryman Fayolle (right) was a thorough, conscientious commander. He rose quickly to an army command, before in November 1917 taking control of French forces in Italy. Returning to France three months later, he assumed command of Reserve Army Group. Privately, he remained sceptical of his superior officer: 'That Foch!' he complained. 'He'll be the death of me!'

Railways and roads were built and improved in the build-up to the battle. Here, work is in full swing at Le Petit Blangy, 22 June 1916. A series of railway sidings were constructed here, 10km south-east of Amiens. On the Albert–Chaulnes line, the site was close to a big railway artillery depot, as well as the junction with lines from Amiens, north to Albert and south to Paris. A further 3km of narrow-gauge sidings were also built at Cérisy, 18km east. Indeed, so many extra lines of all gauges were laid in preparation for the offensive that stocks of rails and sleepers began to run low and extra supplies were requisitioned from private industry. Much of the matériel for railway and trench construction was initially transported by barge, and an unloading facility was created at Bray-sur-Somme for its onward transfer via narrow-gauge tracks.

Pick and shovel in hand, a working party of 'Senegalese' proceed down the Grande Rue, Rosières-en-Santerre, 28 May 1916. The troops were in fact recruited throughout sub-Saharan Africa. French commanders doubted the ability of their African troops to withstand trench warfare, so many battalions were used as working parties rather than as combat troops. In the background are the buildings of Le Familistère, a metalworking enterprise founded in 1880 by Jean-Baptiste Godin. It was run as a workers' co-operative which ploughed its profits into social housing and local schools.

Fresh meat supplies are delivered to front-line units, near Cérisy-Gailly, 28 June 1916. With each man due a daily ration of 450g, an army corps consumed on average 18 tonnes of meat a day, requiring a herd of several hundred animals. Fresh meat was distributed to each army using requisitioned and converted Paris buses. In more active sectors, tinned meat was supplied instead.

A *camion-bazar* stands ready for business, Boves, 11 May 1916. The riverside village of Boves, 10km south-east of Amiens, was a key crossing-point of the Avre, close to its junction with the Somme. The *camion-bazars* were mobile shops run by each regiment on a co-operative basis, providing newspapers, magazines, and food and drink to supplement the plain fare of military rations. As a rule, the shelves were quickly emptied as the vans made their rounds of the rest billets.

Men train to use the new 1916-pattern 37mm gun, whose role was to provide close fire support to the advancing infantry. The gun crew could break down the gun into its component parts (barrel, trail, shield and wheels) and carry them into action. It was a useful weapon, if rather heavy, and crews often left the shield and wheels behind in favour of extra ammunition. The first examples were distributed to training depots in February, and to front-line units in May.

A machine-gunner of 53rd Colonial Infantry poses with his full equipment, Caix, 1916. He is armed with the newly introduced Chauchat machine gun, issued at the rate of eight per infantry company from March 1916. The role of the Chauchat gunner was not to offer precision fire, but to follow the artillery barrage as closely as possible while firing continuously on the enemy trenches, forcing German heads down while his pals crossed no man's land.

A mopper-up of 53rd Colonial Infantry strikes a dramatic pose, Caix, 1916. The moppers-up were essential to French tactics. Rather than risk a lone machine gun or redoubt holding up an assault, the first waves were instructed to press on beyond the German front-line trench to the next objective, leaving knots of resistance to the follow-up waves. The moppers-up were equipped with trench knives, revolvers and grenades. 'This is it,' reported Georges Lafond (22nd Colonial Infantry). 'This time, it's the real thing. The moppers-up are getting their toys, the so-called "Avenger's knife" [for 1870], and we're each getting an extra quart of red wine.'

Right: Pockets bulging with grenades, a bomber of 53rd Colonial Infantry demonstrates proper throwing technique, Caix, 1916. 'For attack or defence at close range, and for patrols, the grenade soon held sway', recalled Jacques Meyer (329th Infantry). 'With its lobbed trajectory, it was the only way of reaching the occupants of trenches protected from flat rifle-fire ... the grenades called "lemons", after their shape, had a cast-iron outer with a raised grid-pattern and were more reliable in use. There was no better way of clearing a captured dugout than a lemon tossed from the top of the steps.'

Men of 62nd Senegalese Tirailleurs practise with their M2 gas masks, Proyart, 24 June 1916. Formed at the southern French base of Fréjus (Var) in March 1916, the 62nd would be attached to 52nd Colonial Infantry – one Senegalese company serving with each of the 52nd's four battalions. The M2 started to reach units in March 1916 and provided five hours of protection to the wearer.

A long 155mm gun is hauled by a Latil TAR, near Le Petit Blangy. The gun's name, 'Vengeuse' (Avenger), is painted on the barrel. The mechanization of the artillery began in 1912 with 4th Heavy Artillery Regiment, but the conflict accelerated the process, and by May 1916 almost 120 batteries were hauled by lorry. The Latil was the workhorse of the heavy artillery; Renault models were used only for the heaviest guns. All guns required modification of their wheels and axles to improve shock absorption. 'There are guns large and small, of every shape, size and calibre', reported Georges Duhamel (Ambulance 9/3). 'From squat little mortars, short and wide-mouthed, like you see on the terrace of the Invalides, to big naval guns, long and slender, tapered like cigars; huge guns of unusual design, on giant platforms, with armoured turrets; strange guns as long as the trains they are mounted on.'

Heavy shells are transported by a narrow-gauge railway laid along the Bray–Chuignes road, near Froissy, 25 June 1916. Coal briquettes are piled on the side tanks of the loco to be used as fuel. 'On the main road from Amiens to Albert', a little further north, journalist Henri Douchet enthusiastically observed another 'two-way stream of cars, lorries, artillery columns and supply convoys. No battlefield had ever been so thoroughly organized or such powerful means of destruction assembled.'

A working party unloads trench mortar bombs, Mézières-en-Santerre, 1916. Jean Rivet (105th Infantry) was part of a similar team: 'On 1 July we left for the rear areas (Rosières-en-Santerre). Our task was unloading the military trains that arrived each day: timber for the trenches, shells of all calibres, Adrian huts. Different teams unloaded day and night. That's where I saw the first 400mm guns, heading for Rosières. After a week I got the leave I'd been waiting for since December 1915. I was glad to get away for a few days. It was heavy work and the food was dreadful.'

A crowd of spectators watch as a 'sausage' prepares for launch, Camp 51, near Chuignes, 1916. The balloon belonged to 75th or 80th Balloon Company, supporting the units of I Colonial Corps. Army and corps aviation commanders were ordered to observe all work in progress within the German lines, the disposition and activities of the enemy artillery, and the density and dispositions of the infantry. To ensure the reports were coordinated and disseminated in a timely manner, senior commanders were also instructed to create a communications network linking army group, army, corps and divisional headquarters.

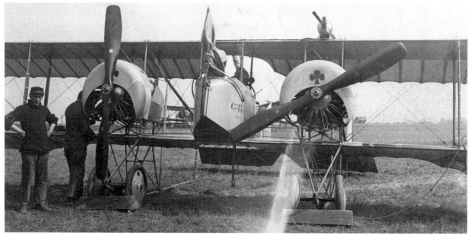

A Caudron G4 prepares for take-off, Sailly-Laurette airfield, 30 April. The crew could communicate with the French artillery via a wireless set powered by the wind-driven generator mounted on the aircraft's upper wing. In his pre-offensive orders, Foch instructed his commanders to 'deploy their aircraft to allow the maximum number to operate simultaneously over the attack zone, without concentrating them to a degree that unduly compromises the effectiveness of the individual machine ... each army must coordinate its use of wireless to allow aircraft so equipped to work in as tight a pack as possible'.

Morlancourt airfield (also known as Bois-des-Tailles) was situated midway between Albert and the Somme. Just visible in the background is the village of the same name. In the foreground are the accommodation huts and transport lines; behind them is a line of easily erected Bessonneau hangars and to the rear are the aircraft. Constructed by Sixth Army in February 1916, Morlancourt was home during the battle to squadrons F24 and F215, joined at various times by C10, F33, F35, F72, F204 and F208 (all Sixth Army), and F41 and C53 (Second Army). The airfield closed at the end of the war.

The celebrated *Cigognes* (Storks) of N3 are briefed by General Fayolle following a medals ceremony, Cachy airfield, 20 June. The audience includes the cream of French fighter pilots, including CO Antonin Brocard (1885–1950), André Chainat (1892–1961), Albert Deullin (1890–1923), René Dorme (1894–1917), Joseph Guiget (1891–1979), Georges Guynemer (1894–1917), Mathieu de La Tour (1883–1917) and Georges Raymond (1897–1918). 'The air battle will be particularly important from the very outset, as the enemy aircraft will be concentrated in the attack zone, intensifying their efforts to spot and follow our preparations, while at the same time launching actions en masse to counter our observation machines. Your task is thus twofold: a. to guarantee freedom of action for friendly observation machines; b. to deny air space to the enemy.'

Infantry arrive by lorry in Suzanne, a riverside village 5km east of Bray. 'Our departure for the Somme came as no surprise,' claimed Paul Dubrulle (8th Infantry). 'We weren't thrown into the furnace without warning, as at Verdun. On the contrary, we were able to watch at our leisure as news came in from distant parts, follow the progress of rumours and orders, and slowly elevate our souls to a pitch equal to the huge effort about to be required of us.'

Bugles sounding, a Senegalese battalion marches past, Place de l'Amiral Courbet, Boves, 20 June 1916. French regiments carried the single-shot 1886 Lebel rifle, but Senegalese troops were issued with the 1907 Berthier – lighter, easier to handle and, crucially, equipped with a three-round magazine. The French were fully aware of the advantages of a magazine rifle, but so great were pre-war stocks of the Lebel that it was only in 1916 that a new rifle, the 1907/15 pattern, was issued to French regiments. This was followed almost immediately by the improved 1916 pattern, raising the capacity of the magazine from three rounds to five.

Having successfully organized road traffic under a single command at Verdun, the French installed a similar system on the Somme. With the main roads north of the river assigned to the British, French troops were supplied via the old Roman road across the Santerre plateau, linking Amiens with Foucaucourt, Estrées and Belloy-en-Santerre. At Proyart, transport columns could branch north for Bray-sur-Somme: a bridging point, railhead, canal port and notorious bottleneck. In this photograph, cars, lorries and horse-drawn wagons cross the Place de la Liberté in both directions. From Bray, the vehicles could fan out to the north and east, including a second crossing at Cappy, 3km distant. At the height of the offensive, 6,600 vehicles a day were travelling along the Bray–Cappy road.

Men of the 2nd Régiment Mixte de Zouaves et de Tirailleurs march through Boves, 21 June 1916. Lieutenant Jacques Meyer of 329th Infantry, a reservist regiment, observed the gathering force: 'We know who they are from their [regimental] numbers, famed for their deeds in Artois, Champagne or Argonne: this is the spearhead, the Division Marocaine, the Corps Colonial, the *chtimis* of 51st Division, the wider family, often scattered but always reconvened on the eve of a solemnity. The quips and shouts fly back and forth, full of the warmth of old friends reunited: "Always the same old who get themselves killed. And the same who bag a cushy number . . ."'

The ammunition column of a chasseurs battalion halts for a meal, Boves, 1916. In 'line' infantry, the column would be equipped with a mixture of two- and four-wheeled carts, but in alpine units, as here, everything was carried by mule. Louis Barthas (296th Infantry) sympathized with their plight: 'Poor beasts!' he commented in November 1916. 'Without shelter of any kind, meek, resigned, tethered in line, they endured the tough conditions, other martyrs . . . with no means to complain, unpitied since they were mere beasts – as if animals and men don't suffer equally. Where were you, Society for the Protection of Animals?'

Infantrymen bivouac alongside the Canal de la Somme, near Éclusier. 'Beneath the line of poplars marching along the valley floor huddled an immense army, with its battalions, animals, vehicles, scrap metal, faded tarpaulins, stinking leather and filth', reported Georges Duhamel (Ambulance 9/3). 'The horses nibbled at the bark of the big trees, which were dying – prey to a premature autumn disease. As if betrayed by the very heavens, a turbulent crowd was trying its best to hide. Three sickly elms served to shelter a whole encampment, a dusty hedge gave shade to the regimental baggage. But with the scant vegetation providing little sanctuary, the army spilled across the bare plain, stripping the roads to the bone, striping the fields with tracks like those formed by the passage of great herds of wild beasts.'

Telephonists, including a number of female civilians, are hard at work at Tenth Army's main exchange, Moreuil, 1916. The number of women employed by the telephone service was growing at this time, from 3,300 early in the century to 46,000 by 1921. Although sometimes less efficient than military lines, civilian lines were frequently used by the army for convenience or speed.

This artillery observation post, Redoubt 99, is spotting for I Colonial Corps artillery, 11 May 1916. The post was situated on the Cappy road, west of Dompierre, with views over that village and the open Santerre plateau. Drawn from 3rd Colonial Regiment and 7th Colonial Regiment, by 27 June I Colonial Corps artillery was creating breaches in the German wire, which it then tried to expand through night-time bombardment. The telephone lines visible in the trench wall above the soldiers' heads connected the post to the group commander, responsible for three batteries. Further lines connected the group CO to his regimental HQ and thence to divisional and corps headquarters. Although vulnerable to enemy shell-fire, they were vital links for commanders.

A battery of 75mm field guns fires a night mission, near Curlu, July 1916. The primary role of the field artillery in the forthcoming offensive was to destroy the enemy wire, although it was also hoped to advance some guns as close support for the infantry during the attack. The 75 was the most famous, and most numerous, artillery piece in the French armoury, but it was unsuited to trench warfare due to its lack of power and a flat trajectory that limited its targets to those in direct line of sight. To compound these failings, the guns were wearing out and proving increasingly prone to explosions caused by faulty ammunition.

Regimental caissons are replenished with 75mm rounds at an ammunition depot, near Harbonnières, June 1916. Georges Duhamel (Ambulance 9/3) had never seen the like: 'And projectiles, projectiles beyond the wildest imagination. Whole fields filled with shells of every calibre, from the minuscule 75s, now looking like toys, to the enormous 400s that need huge jacks to shift them.'

This pile of 75mm shells represents the consumption of just one battery during the last two days of the preliminary bombardment, near Cappy, June 1916. The French calculated that, at a range of 2.5km, 600 HE shells were needed to breach a 25m-deep wire entanglement. Longer ranges required more shells: 1,000 extra shells at a range of 5km; plus another 300 shells for every extra 25m depth of wire.

A short 155C Bange-Filloux opens fire, near Curlu, July 1916. The gun was moved on wheels, but in action it was placed on a hydraulic platform that returned the barrel to the firing position. Within the limits of its range, and aided by trench artillery, medium artillery of this kind (120mm, 155mm and 220mm) was intended to destroy the enemy's defensive works, trenches, machine-gun positions and observation posts. Even so, 80 to 100 rounds would be needed to destroy a bunker of any size.

A 164mm railway gun opens fire, between Caix and Harbonnières, August 1916. In 1914, French artillery doctrine had emphasized mobility and direct fire in preference to howitzers and heavy guns, but the static nature of trench warfare saw older weapons removed from storage and guns developed of ever larger calibre. With aircraft spotting the fall of shot, these enabled the French to strike at the enemy positions at much greater depth. Longer-range artillery like this railway gun were designed to destroy the enemy artillery, and one gun was so allocated for every 250m of front. In total, the French assembled 1,500 guns of all calibres for the offensive, representing one gun for every 28m of front.

This 240mm trench mortar and its crew are positioned on the Santerre plateau, near Marquivillers, April 1916. The 240CT was introduced in 1915 as a counter to the German *minenwerfer*. Proving to be of uncertain accuracy and hard to manoeuvre in the trenches, it was replaced the following year by the 240LT, an improved version with a longer barrel.

A 305mm railway gun opens fire, near Harbonnières, November 1916. Three examples of this weapon were created – named *Anne*, *Marie-Louise* and *Lisette* – using tubes originally intended for the battleship *Iéna*, destroyed in an explosion in 1907. It fired 350kg shells, at a range up to c.25km, and targeted enemy infrastructure such as railway stations.

A shell is loaded into a 280mm mortar, Bray-sur-Somme, 25 June 1916. Sixteen examples of this mortar were constructed before the war, copying a type initially manufactured for export to Russia. By May 1916 enough examples had entered service to equip five separate *groupes*. Firing 205kg shells, at a range up to c.10km, it was used to target the enemy trenches, but it lacked mobility and could be moved only if broken down into four pieces.

A Filloux 370mm howitzer stands ready to fire, near Proyart, 22 June 1916. Only ten examples of this powerful weapon were produced, all during the second half of 1915. Each shell weighed 520kg. 'Dinner time for the Boches', gloated one artilleryman, writing from Foucaucourt in September 1916. 'They'll have fun when this little lot hits them in the chops. That'll give them something to laugh about.'

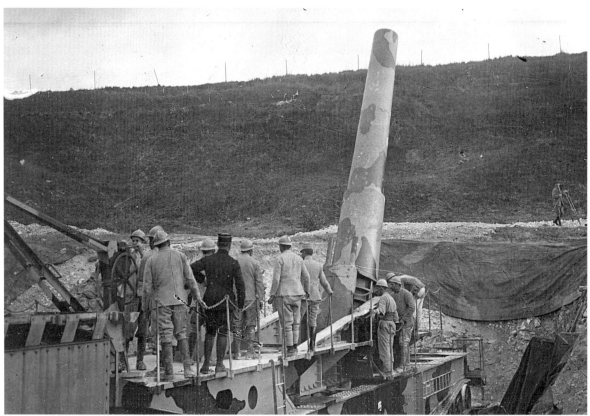

A 400mm howitzer is ready to fire, Harbonnières, 29 June 1916. Each tube was a naval weapon removed from the obsolete coastal battleships *Valmy* and *Brennus* and placed on a railway bogie. In the background, a cameraman waits to film the monster in action.

The bombardment falls in and around Feuillères, June 1916. On the south bank of the Somme, between the second and third objectives of 2nd Colonial Division, this riverside village was obliterated in the fighting. A few kilometres further south, in his billet near Harbonnières, Lieutenant Jacques Meyer (329th Infantry) watched the shelling as he waited for Zero Hour: 'Our bombardment, which had ceased since 3am yesterday, is unleashed again, pounding the edge of the village. It looks like a huge box of pastels is being crushed. The explosions from the 'heavy' 155s and 220s raise eddies of black, ash-grey, red-brown and especially pink from the bricks of the houses; a few hundred metres ahead of the village, a mill-tower is enveloped in pink cloud. Above the ruins, flakes from the greenish or sulphur-yellow balls of the rockets float through the sky.'

The bombardment falls on Curlu and the Chapeau de Gendarme, June 1916. The first objective for 11th Division was Curlu and the forward slope of the ridge to its rear; the second objective was to extend along the ridge and so dominate the reverse slope. The village is largely hidden behind the trees of Bois des Loges. The Germans had made several attempts to establish a post in the wood but all had been driven off by artillery fire.

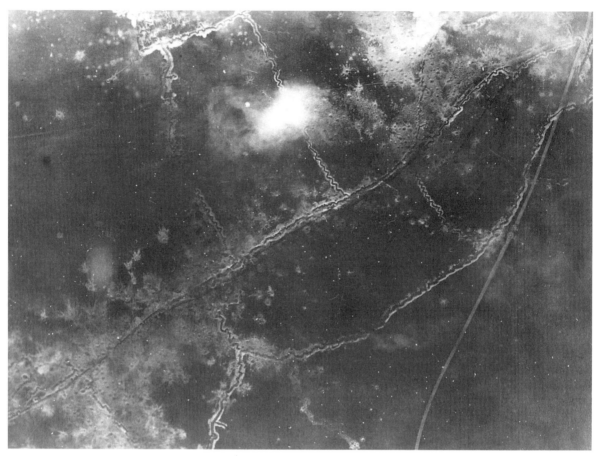

The German Vilbrequin Trench (centre) is targeted by the preliminary bombardment, June 1916. Situated 800m north-west of Curlu, the trench formed a support line behind the Bois Y position, just off picture to the top.

Viewed through a French telescope, a shell bursts in Bois des Loges, June 1916. Author and journalist Pierre Loti recorded his impressions of the bombardment: 'Suddenly towards the east we caught sight of an immense horizon of hills veiled in white smoke . . . the din of a violent thunderstorm . . . This is it, the great battle, the largest the world has ever known, surely the last of its size and one that will leave a dreadful stain on history. This is the battle . . . that will dictate the fate of our race, and that – within our field of vision alone – is costing the lives of 200 men a day.'

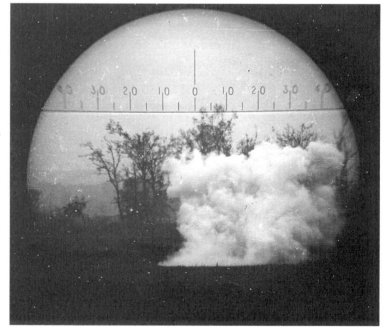

Chapter Three

The Offensive Begins

North of the Somme, in the sector occupied by General Balfourier's XX Corps, the infantry regiments of 39th Division (General Pierre Nourrisson) – 146th, 153rd, 156th and 160th, all Lorrainers from Toul (Meurthe-et-Moselle) – left their trenches at 7.30am on 1 July. Theirs was a difficult task, requiring them to maintain contact on their left with the British, attacking northwards towards Montauban, and on their right with 11th Division (General Eugène Vuillemot), attacking eastwards. Yet within ninety minutes, attacking slightly downhill, the division had captured all its preliminary objectives – Bois Y, Bois Favière, Bois Sans Nom and Bois d'en Haut. German troops attempting to organize a counter-attack from Hardécourt-aux-Bois were caught in the open by French artillery and dispersed. Further progress, however, would depend on the success of the British attacks on Bois de Bernafay and Bois de Trônes. Positioned between 39th Division and the misty valley of the Somme, 11th Division – 26th, 37th, 69th and 79th Infantry regiments – also Lorrainers, from Nancy (Meurthe-et-Moselle) – attacked at the same time, and within thirty minutes much of the German front line lay in their hands. One observation crew reported 37th Infantry making steady progress in most places, although the division was encountering some resistance around Curlu while following the bend of the river south-eastwards. By early evening, however, French patrols had penetrated the village.

Two hours later, the units of General Berdoulat's I Colonial Corps attacked south of the river, with similar success. With its left flank on the Somme, 2nd Colonial Division (General Émile Mazillier) faced an expanding front as it followed the loop of the river north towards Frise and Bois des Loges, while to its right, 3rd Colonial Division (General Martin Gadel, wounded on 2 July and replaced by General Richard Puypéroux) received an even harder nut to crack – the villages of Dompierre and Becquincourt. In the event, the division met little resistance, carrying the entire German front line in a single attempt, and by 11am patrols had reached the enemy second line. Berdoulat was keen to press on, but Fayolle disagreed, insisting on a full artillery preparation. Eventually renewing the attack at 4.30pm, the two divisions fought their way to Herbécourt and Assevillers but were unable to maintain their positions there. Right again, at the southern edge of the battlefield, XXXV Corps retained 53rd Division (General Georges Lebouc) to protect the right flank, leaving 61st Division (General Charles Vandenberg) to attack alone. The 61st's objectives were thus relatively restrained, but included the village of Estrées. Setting off at 9.30am, alongside the adjacent 3rd Colonials, the division made slower progress than its neighbour, losing contact during the afternoon.

On the second day of the offensive, 2nd Colonial Division established itself in Herbécourt, while north-west of the village the Germans evacuated Frise and the loop of the Somme. Stubborn enemy resistance slowed progress both north and south of the river, but concentrated French artillery fire targeted the defenders and allowed the infantry to resume its advance. The men of 3rd Colonial Division reached the outskirts of Assevillers after heavy overnight fighting; patrols despatched by the 2nd Colonials entered Flaucourt, and Berdoulat prepared his cavalry to seize the river crossings. By late on day three, the French had reached and largely secured all their south-bank objectives; on day four they cleared the high ground of the Flaucourt plateau, opening a view across the river to the rooftops of Péronne and the green fields beyond; determined attacks and German withdrawals gave the Moroccan Division (General Alexandre Codet) control of Belloy-en-Santerre; and 53rd Division finally gained a foothold in Estrées.

The French were surprised at their success. General Buat was now commanding 121st Division, part of Sixth Army's reserve: 'The Boches apparently believed our feint on the south bank of the Somme', he confided to his diary. 'Now would be the time to push hard, without worrying too much about maintaining contact, ensuring full artillery support, everything that slows down an advance.' Foch agreed, urging Fayolle to press on while the Germans were in disarray. Yet Fayolle remained cautious, insisting on a pause to consolidate his gains, relieve some of the original first waves and resupply his men and guns. 'Foch gets on my nerves,' he grumbled. 'He's going to make me botch my operation.'

After a pause, extended by twenty-four hours due to rain, the offensive resumed on the south bank on 9 July. Replacing 2nd Colonial Division, 72nd Division (General Louis Ferradini) cleared the south bank of the Somme as far as Biaches, directly opposite Péronne; meanwhile, a kilometre further south, 16th Colonial Division (General François Bonnier) attacked the fortress-farm of La Maisonnette, taking it easily after an intense bombardment dazed and demoralized its defenders. At next-door Barleux, however, the garrison resisted stoutly, and with German resistance stiffening, the French suddenly found themselves pinned in a salient of their own making and struggling to retain their existing gains.

North of the Somme, a joint Franco-British attack was launched on 7 July, with 11th Division targeting the riverside village of Hem. Supported from the south bank by XX Corps and I Colonial Corps artillery, and profiting from early-morning fog, the division almost captured the village in a single rush, but the German defenders clung on until a second bombardment later that day allowed the French to secure the position. Over the next twenty-four hours, the Germans launched five separate counter-attacks, including one that penetrated the French defences only to be immediately bombed out. Meanwhile, at the junction of the French and British armies, 39th Division captured Hardécourt, but could make no further progress after the British failed in their attempt on Bois de Trônes.

Over the next month, the French could make little headway against the German defences, north or south of the Somme. South of the river, small advances were made only after a heavy preliminary bombardment and fierce close-quarters action; German counter-attacks would regain some of the lost ground, only for the whole process to start again. Trapped in a salient, the French were pounded by German artillery ranged on three sides, directed by observers on Mont-Saint-Quentin, across the river, beyond Péronne. By now the pressures of combat, and of supplying men for working parties, were telling on 2nd Colonial Division, particularly 4th Colonial Infantry and 8th Colonial Infantry. On 8 August and the following days, both regiments experienced disturbances, with men refusing to follow orders to fall in. Sixty-two men were charged with abandoning their posts, of whom nineteen were condemned to death; two were subsequently executed, while their comrades were sentenced to terms of hard labour ranging from five to eight years.

New troops were introduced: north of the river, VII Corps (General Georges de Bazelaire); to the south, II Corps (General Denis Duchêne). On the north bank slow but steady progress resumed around Hem, and the stronghold of Ferme de Monacu was finally reduced, making the next objective the intermediate line between Cléry-sur-Somme and Le Forêt (now Leforest). The Germans, however, were now changing their tactics, adopting a deeper, more elastic system of defence in preference to rigidly held trench lines, and enemy reinforcements were also arriving on the Somme. The Allied offensive began to grind to a halt and fresh action would be needed to reinvigorate it.

General Fayolle (centre) reviews 47th Division, Méricourt-sur-Somme, 12 July 1916. Fayolle is flanked by two of his subordinates: left, General Maurice Balfourier (1852–1933), commander of XX Corps; right, General Louis d'Armau de Pouydraguin (1862–1949), commander of 47th Division. After succeeding Foch as commander of XX Corps in 1914, Balfourier remained in post until 17 September 1916, when he transferred to XXXVI Corps; he was relieved in March 1917 and saw no further wartime service. De Pouydraguin commanded 47th Division from March 1915 to August 1917, when he assumed command of XVIII Corps.

These captured German trenches are situated in Bois Y, north of the Moulin de Fargny, near Curlu. Described by one British regimental history as the 'enigmatic sunken Y Wood', the position formed a salient projecting from the German front line. On 1 July, it was among the initial objectives of 79th Infantry: attacking two companies abreast, and in four waves, the wood was secured within twenty minutes.

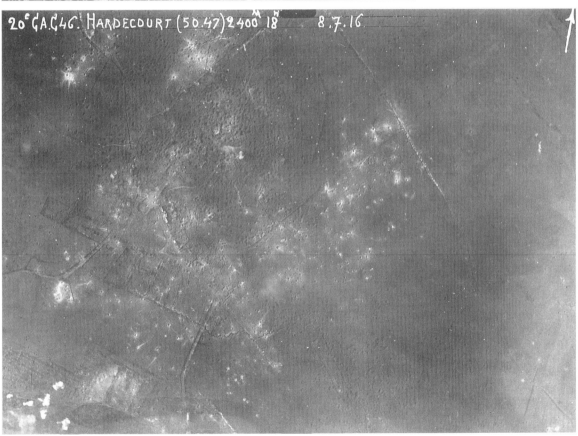

20ᵉ GAC 46. HARDÉCOURT (50.47) 2400 18   8.7.16

An observation flight of C46 records the artillery preparation on Hardécourt-aux-Bois, 8 July 1916. An attack by two regiments – 146th and 153rd Infantry – gained a toehold on the eastern edge of the village after a fierce house-to-house struggle. The rest of Hardécourt finally fell on 15 August, when Franco-British pressure on both flanks forced the Germans to withdraw.

A French soldier examines a heavy Albrecht trench mortar, No. 373575, Curlu, 25 July 1916. The weapon had been abandoned by the German defenders. It had a wooden barrel, bound by wire, and fired a projectile containing 12kg of explosive and 1kg of iron pieces. 'Queer, beastly things', thought British war correspondent Philip Gibbs, 'as primitive as the engines of war used in the fifteenth century'.

Captured German artillery officers and French wounded shelter in a front-line trench, near Curlu, 1 July 1916. The advancing 37th Infantry faced some initial resistance from Bavarian troops, but the regiment carried the position after an 'astonishingly violent' thirty-minute bombardment that left the village in ruins, capturing three officers and 150 men, as well as three machine guns and a trench mortar.

Soldiers clamber through the ruined Moulin de Fargny to refill their canteens from the Somme, 22 July 1916. The buildings were now housing a small French garrison, who maintained an aid post in the basement as well as a forward listening post on the Chapeau de Gendarme, just 30m from the Germans. The position was under constant enemy observation, so reliefs and casualty evacuation could take place only at night.

Viewed from the Chapeau de Gendarme, a bombardment hits the new French positions above Curlu, July 1916. Between 6pm and 6.30pm, on the evening of 1 July, attempts by German defenders to hold out in Eulenberg Quarry had been met with a barrage of 500 heavy artillery shells (155mm–290mm) and 6,000 75mm shells. The French infantry occupied the position unopposed.

French soldiers stop for a meal on the edge of Curlu, 25 July 1916. Cook Jules Maincave (90th Infantry) was famed for his 'beefsteaks dits d'attaque' (attack steaks), well doused in the regimental-issue spirits, as well as a cheese fondue featuring a similarly liberal dose of ration wine. Maincave's renown reached General Henri Gouraud (1867–1946), commander of Fourth Army, who was treated to 'a smooth pâté, heavily seasoned'. To universal sorrow, Maincave was killed near Combles on 30 October.

A company of reinforcements advance through the ruins of Curlu, 30 July 1916. Reliefs were seldom straightforward, as Pierre MacOrlan (269th Infantry) discovered: 'The equipment cuts into the shoulders, the pack presses on the neck, the rifle is shifted to the other shoulder. Our bulging haversacks get in the way in the narrower sections. We meet some machine-gunners with their crates and guns. It's the final straw. The two columns are swallowing each other. We do our best to flatten ourselves against the trench walls to let the machine-gunners through. If those using this communications trench are the relief coming out of the line, all will be friendly enough ... A faint aroma of fresh apples, of fruit drops, catches our throats. More of the tear gas lingering in the holes. We check that we have our gas masks handy.'

Soldier Mathieu Jouy, 22nd Colonial Infantry receives the Légion d'Honneur from General Joffre, near Aubigny, late August 1916. On 1 July, armed with a Chauchat machine gun, Jouy had single-handedly captured several German positions, having previously earned the Médaille Militaire for his gallantry at Beauséjour (Marne) during the Champagne offensive in February 1915. He died in 1965, aged 74.

General Pierre Berdoulat (1861–1930), commander of I Colonial Corps, inspects French 120mm guns, near Cappy, 8 July 1916. The guns had been captured at Maubeuge (Nord) in 1914 and recently recovered; I Colonial Corps was leading the attack south of the river. An experienced colonial solder in Africa and the Far East, and Director of Colonial Troops in 1914, Berdoulat returned to the field that October and was appointed to I Colonial Corps the following April. He transferred to XX Corps in July 1917 and remained there for the rest of the war. Fayolle found his subordinate particularly exasperating: 'I can't stop I Colonial Corps biting off more than they can chew', he wrote on 2 July. 'Instead of directing the battle, Berdoulat has let his divisional commanders have their heads.' On 4 July, with French forces approaching Belloy-en-Santerre and Estrées, Fayolle was at the end of his tether: 'telephone conversation with Berdoulat, [as] pompous and uncomprehending [as ever]. He's wasting my time . . . on a purely practical matter concerning the billets.'

French attackers have taken over a German salvage point for cartridges, cans, canteens and other metal waste, Herbécourt, 15 July 1916. The men are identifiable as colonial troops by the anchor on the helmet badge, and as medical troops by their collar patches, a caduceus within a wreath.

A French soldier views captured German front-line trenches, near Dompierre, 5 July 1916. Signboards point to the Emden Weg (top), a first-aid post (bottom right) and Trench 27 (bottom left). The village had housed the HQ of the German 121st Division. Too thinly spread along the line to be effective, the 121st was withdrawn, exhausted, and from 8 July began transferring to the Ukraine. Charles Barberon (121st Heavy Artillery) passed through Dompierre several days later: 'Until today, I had never witnessed quite such desolation. Not a house in the village remains intact. On more careful examination I could spot only one chimney. Nearly every roof has caved in. A lot of the walls have collapsed. Where the bombardment was particularly heavy, the buildings are reduced to rubble. In some places the shell-holes are so huge, so tightly packed, that it's impossible to tell what used to be there. Anyone with a house will never find where it stood. A few trees are still standing, but most of the branches have been torn off by shellbursts, and nearly all the leaves scorched by gas.'

General Fayolle (right) watches from the roadside as a colonial infantry column moves up the line, Dompierre, 5 July 1916. Fayolle, who liked to view the terrain in person, earning the nickname General Duckboard (*Caillebottis*) for the frequency of his visits to the trenches, was satisfied with this inspection, 'terrible destruction, not many bodies'. The following day brought another visitor: 'Joffre was here. He already scents victory and is keen to bring up the cavalry.'

German prisoners pressed into service help French wounded to the rear, near Herbécourt, 9 July 1916. Crossing the Santerre plateau, Raphaël Weill (Ambulance 3/3) found 'a line of helmeted gendarmes barring the crossing-points, men and transport weaving along a track crossing the burned, roasted, shredded plain, not a tree, nor a flower, nor a blade of grass, flayed to the bone by the shells'.

Laden with pack, rifle, ammunition and personal equipment – a c.25kg load – troops march past a calvary and sugar works, west of Dompierre, 4 July 1916. Producing beet sugar was an important industry throughout Picardy, with no less than 166 such factories in the region before the war. Like the rest of Dompierre, this sugar works – the Sucrerie Normande – was completely destroyed in the fighting.

This battery of long 120mm guns fires from its position between Assevillers and Belloy-en-Santerre, 2 August 1916. As an anchor of the German second line south of the Somme, Assevillers formed one of 3rd Colonial Division's second objectives. Although reported to be strongly held, it fell on 2 July and the following day was put into a state of defence by the Foreign Legion's Régiment de Marche.

French soldiers surround civilian Émile Villement, Belloy-en-Santerre, 5 July 1916. Having remained in the heavily fortified village during the German occupation, Villement is about to be evacuated following its liberation by the French. Right, a soldier from 8th Zouaves de Marche proudly displays his Croix de Guerre; centre is a member of 4th Tirailleurs de Marche; and left, an Engineer.

The ruins of Belloy-en-Santerre, November 1916. The village had fallen on 4 July to members of the Foreign Legion, including American poet Alan Seeger (1888–1916), a Harvard classmate of T S Eliot and the uncle of folk singer Pete Seeger. 'The first section (Alan's section) formed the right and vanguard of the company and mine formed the left wing', recalled Seeger's comrade Rif Baer. 'After the first bound forward, we lay flat on the ground, and I saw the first section advancing beyond us and making toward the extreme right of the village of Belloy-en-Santerre. I caught sight of Seeger and called to him, making a sign with my hand. He answered with a smile. How pale he was! His tall silhouette stood out on the green of the cornfield. He was the tallest man in his section. His head erect, and pride in his eye, I saw him running forward, with bayonet fixed. Soon he disappeared and that was the last time I saw my friend.'

American legionnaires pose outside at their billets, Froissy (Oise), January 1917. 'They were hard men and discipline was harsh,' wrote fellow legionnaire Blaise Cendrars. 'They were professionals.' The Foreign Legion's Régiment de Marche suffered appalling casualties during the assault on Belloy-en-Santerre: 112 men were killed, 488 wounded and 131 reported missing during the capture of the village.

A battalion of 352nd Infantry heads to rest, Belloy-en-Santerre, 2 August 1916. In the front line since 13 July, the 352nd had also suffered heavily in the attacks around Belloy, losing some 220 officers and men as casualties in attacks on the southern edge of the village.

The German positions were heavily fortified. Here, stretcher-bearers rest beside a German 105mm howitzer inside a concrete emplacement destroyed by French artillery, near Estrées, 10 July 1916. Second left, a man holds a reel of signal cable. Jacques Meyer (329th Infantry) described bombing his way into the enemy trenches: 'Off we went, but not using the steps we'd dug earlier. We started off slowly, taking infinite care, along the communications trench. The vanguard destroyed the barricade behind which two or three Boches lay splayed across the trench ... Next we cleared a path with our grenades, which exploded with a crack that rang through the air or with a dull thud if dropped in the shelters. From our departure trench, [the] machine-gun section covered our advance with a hail of bullets, some skimming the parapet and keeping heads down.'

The French brought forward their artillery to provide close support for the attack on the second and third objectives: this 90mm gun is positioned among the ruins of Fay church. 'Dreadful!' exclaimed Marcel Étévé (417th Infantry). 'I've seen the results of our artillery preparation. Of the whole village, all that can be seen are fragments of walls, scarcely a metre [high]. The plateau where it stood is just a succession of shell-holes, adjoining or overlapping; not a square metre of ground is untouched. The houses have disappeared completely.' Fayolle, however, was unhappy with his men: 'the troops are completely unsuited to a war of movement, especially the artillery. And the heavy artillery is terrible burden to drag around.'

French soldiers settle into a comfortable German officers' dugout, complete with piano, Bois des Satyres, west of Estrées, 9 August 1916. The officers of Bavarian Pionier-Regiment Nr. 10 had enjoyed similar conditions in nearby Flaucourt, where Raphaël Weill (Ambulance 3/3) and his chums found 'a well-stocked library, tables strewn with German newspapers amid boxes still filled with cigars, huge glasses and stoneware tankards with a layer of sour beer in the bottom. We had a good rummage round as the soldier on campaign becomes a bit of a second-hand goods dealer; we looked like a gang of thieves.'

Triumphant chasseurs à pied scrape the mud from their boots, Feuillères, 23 July 1916. Introduced into the line as part of the follow-up wave when the offensive resumed on 9 July, pressing on towards Biaches, 72nd Division included two chasseur battalions, 56th and 59th. Feuillères, and the adjoining crossing over the Somme had fallen to a mixed European-Senegalese battalion of 36th Colonial Infantry around 5pm on 3 July.

French troops look east from the outskirts of Biaches towards the German lines, 7 August 1916. The Somme and its adjoining canal lie in the middle ground. French progress was halted by the German positions in and around the white house in the trees, on the left of the photograph. To the right are the houses of Sainte-Radegonde, a *faubourg* of Péronne.

Wounded men from 164th Infantry head to the rear along the Cappy road after the capture of Biaches, 9 July 1916. Tied to a buttonhole, each man has a large label affixed by the regimental aid post, detailing the preliminary diagnosis and treatment provided. Its colour denoted the gravity of the case: do not move (blue), convalescent (white), light wound (green + ZA), serious wound (green + ZI). Georges Duhamel (Ambulance 9/3) recalled: 'one little fellow with his arm in a sling. The doctor consulted his notes. "So, you've a wound in your right arm?" he said. "No, it's not a wound," replied the man modestly. "Just a hole."'

A Chauchat gunner takes careful aim from a trench, near the Place de la Mairie, Biaches, 7 August 1916. The enemy is just 30m away. To the right of the gunner is his number two, whose task was to monitor the ammunition supply through the apertures in the sides of the magazine and load a full replacement as soon as the old one was exhausted.

With the French just across the river, the streets of occupied Péronne are quiet, August 1916. The Germans had evacuated most of the civilian population eastwards, to Hannapes (Aisne). Looking north-east over the Grande Place and the town hall, this panorama was taken from the tower of the sixteenth-century church of Saint-Jean-Baptiste, an obvious artillery observation post. The church was also used as temporary housing for Allied prisoners before their transfer to the rear. The first shells had struck the church on 7 July; by the end of the war only a couple of walls were left standing.

French and British prisoners are loaded onto trains, Péronne, July 1916. The captives have attracted a crowd of onlookers, including a military policeman (left) and a member of the German Red Cross (rear, in the darker uniform). Irma Pillois lived in occupied Saint-Quentin, 30km further east. 'At eight o'clock yesterday evening more French prisoners turned up, forty-seven, plus one Englishman, still on foot', notes her diary on 13 July. 'Rumour has it they were captured at La Maisonnette, across the river from Péronne. They almost all have beards. They look very old and tired. Like yesterday's arrivals, they were escorted by lance-armed dragoons.'

Situated in a quarry close to the fortress-farm of La Maisonnette, these former German positions fell easily on 10 July to men of 16th Colonial Division. A fierce bombardment had obliterated the farm, leaving what one German regimental history described as 'nothing but a great field of corpses'. Fayolle had explained the French success quite simply: 'the [Germans] were probably all in the shelters, as usual under a bombardment, so no one was left on guard. That's what normally happens. The Boches turn up unnoticed. And of course we do likewise.'

Men of 47th Division are presented with their medals, near Aubigny, 4 August 1916. Among them is Corporal Jean-Marie Goutaudier (11th Alpine Chasseurs), who is receiving the Légion d'Honneur (an award normally reserved for officers) for his bravery in the follow-up attacks on Hem-Monacu. On 20 July, his battalion lost nearly two-thirds of its effectives during an assault on Bois de Hem. Yet, with his comrade Chasseur Guillot, killed 'because of his courage and fearlessness', Goutaudier captured over 100 prisoners, including two officers. 'It was nothing special', he later claimed. 'Once you're there, you know, you just go all out.' Goutaudier died in 1949.

A 37mm infantry gun platoon makes its way forward, near Hem-Monacu, 30 July. The steep slopes of the Chapeau de Gendarme provided good shelter from the German artillery and soon housed many soldiers in a variety of caves and dugouts. 'The spectacle before me really is a quaint one,' wrote Paul Tézenas du Montcel (102nd Territorials): 'Everywhere, along the cliff dominating the right bank of the canal, on the neighbouring hillsides screening us from the enemy, are dug *gourbis*, *cagnas*, *guitounes*, shelters of every shape and size. It looks like a huge native village mixed up with a settlement of cave dwellers.'

A wounded man awaits evacuation, Hem-Monacu, 30 July 1916. The 2nd Régiment Mixte de Zouaves et Tirailleurs was attached to 41st Division for the assault on Ferme de Monacu; attacking in heavy mist, they met initially with mixed success until a supporting attack by 229th Infantry, from Feuillères, south of the river, took the Germans by surprise. The farm eventually fell the next day. The 2nd RMZT suffered nearly 400 casualties during the operation, taking almost 100 prisoners from the Saxons of Infanterie-Regiment Nr. 101 and Infanterie-Regiment Nr. 102.

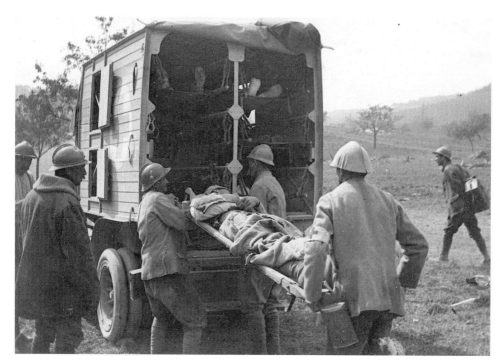

Loading stretcher-cases into a racked ambulance, Hem-Monacu, 30 July 1916. Jacques Meyer (329th Infantry) visited a field hospital behind the lines in Harbonnières: 'I've just had a vision of unforgettable grandeur. I entered the church and this is what I saw: in the nave, aisles and transept, the chairs are replaced by neat rows of stretchers, their occupants renewed constantly by the stream of ambulances pulling up before the porch. Around them bustle the doctors in white smocks. Near the choir stalls are some Boches, their [grey] uniforms now green, waiting their turn to be bandaged. In the chiaroscuro of the church, itself deserving of a Rembrandt, the white bandages, red blood and blue tunics meld imperceptibly in a peerless tricolour harmony, and the faces, grubby or pale, framed by heavy beards, emerge from the sombre depths like the ashen Christs of the Spanish school.'

An artillery observer perches in a tree, Suzanne, 9 August 1916. Just behind the front lines, the seventeenth-century château here housed a French headquarters. To south and east, the woods had been largely destroyed in the fighting. So too on the opposite bank, between Éclusier and Frise, where Raphaël Weill (Ambulance 3/3) found Bois de la Vache reduced to shreds: 'A few shattered tree-trunks twist their sorry branches above earth burned, scorched, turned upside down by a cataclysm'.

This aerial view of Maurepas was taken by a XX Corps observation crew, 21 July 1916. On a spur overlooking French lines, the photograph shows the centre and eastern side of this north-bank village. The line of craters (left) marks the old German line, known to the French as the Tranchée des Moustiques (Mosquito Trench). Maurepas finally fell on 24 August, after twelve days of fighting.

German trenches are under bombardment, Bois des Croisettes, near Cléry-sur-Somme, 12 August 1916. The men of 60th Infantry captured the wood that same day, taking twenty-three enemy prisoners, before advancing alongside 40th Infantry to within 500–600m of the village, beside the north bank of the Somme. The wood is now the site of the cemetery of Cléry-sur-Somme, which contains the graves of 2,332 French soldiers.

German prisoners are gathered in a holding camp, Longueau, 1 August 1916. At the junction of several railway lines leading south, Longueau was a useful holding area for prisoners. In the first week of July alone, the French captured 9,000 Germans. 'Here come the first *Kamaraden*, ragged, ashen-faced, with a greenish pallor – the result of fatigue, hunger and the horror of dreadful hours under bombardment', observed Jacques Meyer (329th Infantry). 'Marching between a hedge of blue tunics, amid curious stares and silence, many of these Saxons and Brandenburgers must be adults, but their real age is hard to discern. Some look like old men, diminished and shrunken; others seem as weak as infants . . . An old territorial and a colonial from the class of '15 . . . both hit in the hand, escort a Boche with a leg wound, masking their concern beneath a show of brusqueness, although the colonial hasn't passed up the chance to half-inch his [prisoner's] canteen.'

Interpreters were used to interrogate the prisoners. Here, Lieutenant Georges Weill (1882–1970) is pictured in camp, Cérisy-Gailly, 2 July 1916. Weill had served in the Reichstag as a deputy for occupied Metz (Moselle), but left secretly on the outbreak of war to join the French army. After the war, he returned to political life, serving in the French parliament as a deputy for the *département* of Bas-Rhin, and on committees working on the reintegration of newly liberated Alsace-Lorraine.

More German prisoners are loaded aboard a train transferring them to the interior, Longueau, 1 August 1916. Described as part of the conscription class of 1916, which had been called to the colours between August and November 1915, these men certainly appear very young. By the time the Somme offensive got under way, many of the class of 1917 had also been mobilized.

Lieutenant Albert Deullin (N3) zeroes in the synchronized Vickers gun of his Nieuport fighter, Cachy, 10 September 1916. Having scaled back their assault on Verdun, the Germans were once again challenging for air superiority. '[Early in] the [Somme] offensive, the lone single-seater was king', observed Deullin, a noted aerial tactician. '[Large] patrols served only to drive away the enemy. Everything fled as they approached, then returned when they left, so they hardly downed a single Boche. By contrast the lone single-seater could stalk his prey, conceal himself more easily in sun, mist or cloud, exploit his opponent's blind spots, and launch lightning strikes impossible for a large patrol. Gradually, however, the situation changed. Learning from experience, the enemy coordinated his efforts and introduced impeccably disciplined two-seater and single-seater patrols . . . After several unsuccessful and sometimes painful experiences, our fighters had to admit that the days of the lone wolf were over. We had to find an alternative.' After a series of experiments, led by Deullin, the French eventually settled on the three-man patrol.

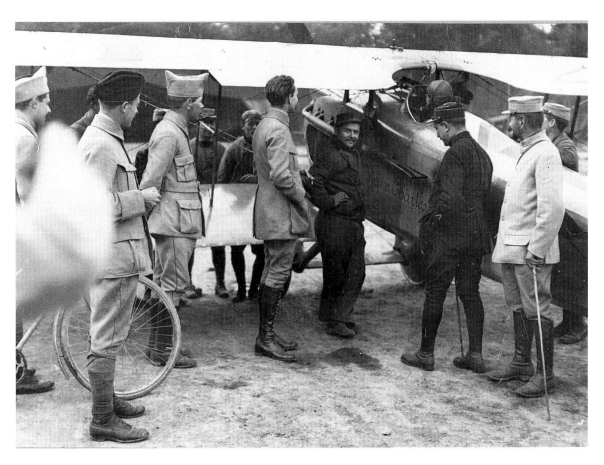

Lieutenant Georges Guynemer (N3) returns in triumph in his first SPAD 7, Cachy, 15 September 1916. The ace has just achieved his sixteenth victory, a Rumpler C of FA8b, shot down near Saint-Cren. His SPAD, 'Vieux Charles', offered an improvement over the Nieuport, and was his sixth plane of that name. It was delivered on 27 August, only to be hit by French anti-aircraft fire on 23 September and written off. 'The role of the aviation service in battle goes beyond simple observation missions,' Foch encouraged his crews. 'Its tenacity and élan give us the moral advantage over the enemy. Not only does it permit commanders to see "what's happening on the ground", it is idolized, its every move closely followed, by the front-line troops, so its daring bolsters their morale and convinces them of the superiority of our matériel.'

Lieutenant Deullin (left) chats to a fellow N3 pilot, Adjudant Paul Tarascon, Cachy, 30 September 1916. Meanwhile a mechanic works on the plane. In the centre of the upper wing are the two semi-circular brackets used by the pilot to haul himself in and out of the cockpit. Between the brackets is the mounting for a Lewis gun, replaced here by the Vickers mounted on the engine cowling. Flying on escort duties, Tarascon had recently tangled with the aces of Jasta 2, including the Red Baron, Manfred von Richthofen: 'He passed just a couple of metres below my wing, raising his arm in greeting as he did so! . . . It was breathtaking. I can picture him now saluting me in his black balaclava. We were both out of ammunition . . . and I wanted to withdraw without seeming to run away. I banked and pointed my Lewis gun into the air so he could see it. Then we each flew off to our own side.'

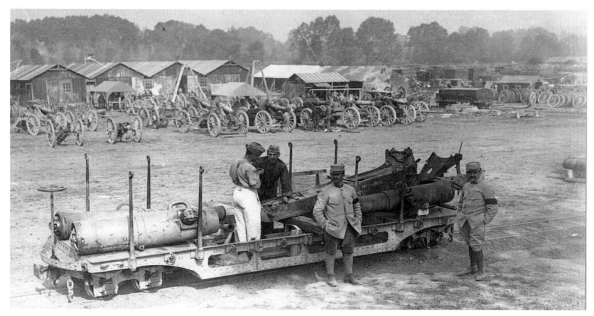

Damaged artillery pieces arrive by narrow-gauge railway for repair at Northern Army Group's artillery park, La Neuville-Sire-Bernard, 30 July 1916. On the river Avre, south-east of Amiens, the village became an important junction of narrow- and standard-gauge railway lines. It was also home to a lines of communication hospital, as well as Field Ambulance 1/9.

Members of the newly created Camouflage Section receive their medals, Amiens, August 1916. Left is the unit's CO, Lieutenant Lucien-Victor Guirand de Scévola (1871–1950), an artist noted for his pastel portraits; centre is Jean-Louis Forain (1852–1931), Inspector of Camouflage; and right, landscape painter Louis Abel-Truchet (1857–1918). Scévola never went near the front but, for his role in 'developing the army's camouflage procedures', was awarded the Croix de Guerre. Charles Barberon (121st Heavy Artillery) spoke for many of his comrades: 'I've always felt the Croix de Guerre is handed out indiscriminately. Some really deserving soldiers never get one. At Flaucourt, three drivers brought up a munitions wagon. One was killed, another seriously wounded. The third looked after his comrade and returned with all the horses. He never received any praise for his deeds. He never got a thing. In contrast, many of the soldiers who have citations merit them little or not at all.'

Probe in hand, a dentist treats a patient in a mobile surgery, between Ignaucourt and Mézières-en-Santerre, 28 September 1916. The army was slow to introduce a dental service; it was formally established in the spring of 1916, with dentists to be attached to individual field ambulances. While doctors ranked as officers, qualified dentists came lower down the pecking order, equated only with warrant officers (*adjudants*). This particular mobile surgery was the gift of the Oeuvre d'Assistance aux Dépôts d'Éclopés, a charity that aided convalescent hospitals.

This temporary lines of communication hospital occupies a site constricted by the winding valley of the river Luce, Cayeux-en-Santerre, 21 September 1916. Also housing six field ambulances, a mobile surgical unit, Autochir 20, and a railway station, the hospital could accommodate 1,600 patients – 400 walking wounded, 400 seated, 300 lying down and 500 convalescent. A hospital train transferred the most seriously wounded men to base and civilian hospitals every five days.

Chapter Four

Regaining Momentum

By early September 1916, French and British headquarters staff had formulated their plans and relaunched their stalled offensive. The process was not without difficulties, and recriminations were rife on both sides. The French were disappointed by the British lack of progress, blaming tactics disparaged as 'juvenile' by Fayolle. 'It's taken them 120,000 men just to capture three or four villages,' he confided to his diary, 'and there are plenty more [of those] before you reach the Rhine.' Meanwhile General Pierre des Vallières (1868–1918), the French head of mission at Haig's HQ, emerged gloomily from a meeting on 8 September:

> The very different concepts of battle held by French and British commanders make it hard to coordinate French and British operations. While, during each action, we aim to exploit all successes as fully as possible, the British set short-range objectives and never dare push on. This is due to the inflexibility of the British character and their commanders' lack of initiative . . . The British are seeking any pretext to postpone their main offensive for as long as possible, but the reasons remain unknown to me. Just now, they're trying to use the delay in Sixth Army's operations.

Haig was equally scornful, writing on 14 September:

> The fact is that the French infantry is very poor now and lacks the offensive spirit . . . such progress as the French have made has been achieved against a much smaller concentration of artillery [than that opposing the British] and judging by a comparison of the German prisoners working on the roads, those taken by the French are very much inferior in physique.

The British were reluctant to adopt techniques like counter-battery fire plans introduced so successfully in the French sector. And, as Haig had refused to serve under Joffre's orders, the two senior French commanders, Joffre and Foch, had no means of compelling their allies to take joint action; all they could do was to coax.

The main focus of the newly negotiated plan lay north of the Somme: two British armies would make a two-stage attack northwards, coordinating their effort with a similar attack by Sixth Army, initially against the Cléry-Le Forêt line, then against the line running in front of Rancourt to the river. On the south bank, Foch took the opportunity to introduce Tenth Army (General Joseph Micheler) to his right flank, widening the offensive by attacking south-eastwards between Barleux and Chilly. Fayolle was feeling under pressure: 'Foch will drive me like a brute', he complained. 'He doesn't listen to a word I say. The man has never got on with any of his generals.' A visit from Joffre was needed to smooth ruffled feathers: 'You're the best of my army commanders,' Fayolle was reassured.

On the north bank, XX Corps was replaced by I Corps (General Adolphe Guillaumat), with XXXIII Corps (General Alphonse Nudant), newly arrived from Verdun, positioned closer to the river. The French attacked on 3 September and took the German lines with ease: rather than follow a pre-set timetable imposed by HQ, the infantry advanced behind a rolling barrage controlled flexibly by the leading waves via a sophisticated system of visual signals, while Cléry was also targeted by a machine-gun barrage from across the river. By evening, the French had penetrated up to 3km into the enemy positions: Le Forêt lay in their hands, leaving just a few isolated groups in Cléry for mopping up the next day. From 4 to 6 September the men of XXXIII Corps built on this success, seizing the village of Omiécourt, south of Cléry, rushing a series of positions in woods in front of the German third line, then pausing to bring forward their guns.

Now, however, the offensive stalled. Bad weather was compounded, as so often happened on the Western Front, by logistical problems in the rear, and any further action was delayed for another six days. On 12 September, at 12.30pm, the assault was renewed on the German third position, targeting the villages of Bouchavesnes, Rancourt and Sailly-Saillisel, plus the artillery position on Mont-Saint-Quentin, overlooking Péronne. Attacking along a three-corps front, I Corps, VII Corps and XXXIII Corps (left to right) made steady progress, capturing Bouchavesnes and a 6km stretch of the German trenches. With success in sight, the cavalry was ordered forward, but once again confusion and congestion in the lines of communication frustrated the attack. The French were too slow to exploit the potential breach, and the new salient was easily contained by the German artillery and machine guns. Blame for the chaos in the rear areas fell on General Nudant, who was subsequently sacked.

South of the river, the three corps comprising Micheler's Tenth Army – II Corps (Duchêne), X Corps (General François Anthoine) and XXXV Corps (Jacquot) – were responsible for widening the offensive southwards in the hope of forcing a victory. They attacked on 4 September along a 17km front; but with Verdun still draining men and matériel, resources were running low. The preliminary six-day bombardment was less intense than that of June and July, some enemy wire remained uncut and the counter-battery fire was also less effective. The more experienced formations in II Corps made the greatest gains, but the offensive as a whole met with mixed results, and within days it had degenerated into a slogging match, each minor victory achieved only at the price of heavy casualties.

Foch, however, was sufficiently heartened by French progress, and a British advance on 15 September at Flers-Courcelette, to order further small-scale attacks, keeping the enemy off-balance by nibbling away at positions scattered all along the front line. North of the river, Sixth Army made little ground in these hurriedly arranged actions; to the south, however, Tenth Army secured three more villages: Berny, Vermandovillers and Deniécourt. On 25 September, Sixth Army, now heavily reinforced, tried again: Rancourt and Frégicourt both fell into French hands, and in a notable example of Franco-British cooperation, the village of Combles was outflanked to east and west and captured.

General Adolphe Guillaumat (1863–1940) was the commander of I Corps, whose men renewed the attack north of the river. With extensive staff experience, and popular with Radical politicians, Guillaumat was later promoted to several army commands, including Second Army (December 1916), the Allied Army of the Orient (December 1917) and Fifth Army (1918). In the 1920s, he drafted the final plans for what became the Maginot Line and commanded the Allied armies in the Occupied Rhineland.

An artillery observation post is set up in an old trench, Ferme de l'Hôpital, near Le Forêt, September 1916. 'Personally, I would make all the gun-crew in my section take turns to accompany me when I go with a telephonist on observation in the front line,' insisted Ivan Cassagnau (6th Artillery). 'Infantrymen need to feel visited, admired even, by the other arms of service.'

The shattered remains of Cléry-sur-Somme, late September 1916. The village had fallen on 3 September. After losing 640 men in August around Hem, and spending a fortnight at rest around Villers-Bretonneux, 363rd Infantry returned to the fray at Cléry. The regiment captured its first objective, taking almost 1,200m of ground and 300 prisoners, but lost a similar number of men in the action. Returned to strength, it was transferred away from the Somme to another sector of the front.

A carrier pigeon is prepared at 60th Infantry HQ, Carrière, 12 September 1916. The regiment is about to go into action, supporting the attack of 44th Infantry in Bois des Ouvrages, which resulted in the capture of Bouchavesnes. The regimental number is visible on the sandbag (centre). The man in the dark uniform is an artillery liaison officer, while far right is a signaller.

An assault wave digs in, Ferme Labbé, south of Bouchavesnes, 25 September 1916. Batteries of 84th Heavy Artillery fired over 500 rounds in support of the attack on 12 September, and the village fell within two hours. The instructions issued before the September attacks specified the make-up and spacing of the attacking waves: first would come the assault wave, consisting of a half platoon of bombers and Chauchat gunners; the second wave, composed of VB rifle grenadiers and riflemen, would follow about ten to fifteen paces behind; finally, at a further ten to twenty paces, the moppers-up would bring up the rear. The soldiers in the attacking line would be spaced at intervals of four to five paces, a gap proved during the opening phase of the offensive to produce a notable reduction in casualties without disrupting unit cohesion.

General Denis Duchêne (1862–1950) commanded II Corps at Verdun and on the Somme. 'It's increasingly clear that this man is a bit of a bully,' commented General Buat (121st Division). 'He's already acquired a pretty poor reputation within the division, although I never have any trouble with him.' Duchêne was promoted in December 1916 to the command of Tenth Army, which suffered huge losses on the Chemin des Dames and played a prominent role in the subsequent unrest. Having transferred to Sixth Army in December 1917, Duchêne would be summarily dismissed in May 1918 for battlefield failures during the German spring offensive.

General Joseph Micheler (1861–1931) receives the insignia of a Commander of the Légion d'Honneur from President Raymond Poincaré, Château de Moreuil, 30 September 1916. A sound if unspectacular leader, Micheler (far left) took command of Tenth Army in April 1916, after a rise attributed in some quarters to his political connections. In April 1917 he commanded Reserve Army Group during the catastrophic Chemin des Dames offensive, transferring to Fifth Army the following month. Alongside him is General François Anthoine (1860–1944), a pre-war staff officer who had commanded X Corps (Tenth Army) since September 1915. Promoted to the command of First Army in 1917, Anthoine later transferred to Fourth Army before returning to GQG as chief of staff. Both Micheler and Anthoine fell abruptly in the wake of the German spring offensive in 1918: Micheler for failures of battlefield command after his troops were overrun by the enemy; Anthoine as a scapegoat from the headquarters staff.

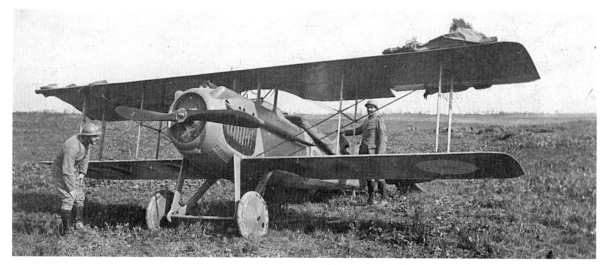

Wounded by ground fire, Lieutenant Georges Pelletier d'Oisy (1892–1953) has landed his SPAD just inside French lines, near Flaucourt, 10 October 1916. Pelletier d'Oisy, nicknamed 'Pivolo', had transferred to aviation from the cavalry in 1912 and was credited with five victories while serving with HF19, MS12 (alongside the ace Jean Navarre) and N/SPA69. After the war he became famous for a long-distance flight between Paris and Tokyo in 1924.

The fortress village of Chilly is under attack, 4 September 1916. The French had been hammering at this position at the southern edge of the battlefield since 8 August. Most of the terrain shown here was captured in the first wave by 25th Infantry, but the defenders were sheltering in an extensive network of tunnels beneath the village and it took another week to prise them out. The village was finally declared captured on 10 September.

This aid post, marked PS (poste de secours), occupies a corner of Lihons, 1 September 1916. Centre, in the dark uniform, is a padre. Each divisional ambulance unit was officially allowed one padre on its strength; elsewhere regimental colonels often permitted priests serving as private soldiers to minister to their comrades. Achille Liénart (201st Infantry), a teacher at a seminary in Cambrai (Nord), took part in August in an attack near Maurepas: 'I spent the morning in the sunken lane offering communion and hearing confession for anyone who wanted it. When I was done, my lads gave me their letters, for many perhaps their last. Before going into action, they wrote as best they could, in pencil, on their knees. They mentioned all their loved ones and were anxious that the letters were posted. I took a good 300 to the aid post at Hardécourt.'

Following their regimental colour, the men of 2nd Infantry advance into the German front line, near Chilly, 4 September 1916. Their objective was Côte 86. The moments before the assault waves went over the top were unbearably fraught. Louis Botti (1st Zouaves) took part in an attack on Bois d'Anderlu, near Combles, on 12 September: 'Two shells burst in front of the parallel . . . The men duck . . . Have the Boches spotted us? Is the bombardment under way? No, the firing has stopped. It's time to go . . . This is it! The CO clambers from the trench . . . Forward . . . Well aligned, holding their weapons aloft, the tirailleurs follow at walking pace . . . de Boissieu is on my left, Lachaise on my right. A swing to the right turns the first wave towards its objective. We scale some rising ground . . . We're on the plateau . . .'

Curious British and French onlookers gather in rain and mud to view a tank, Ferme de Bronfay, near Maricourt, 29 September 1916. The Allies had high hopes of this new British weapon, which had made its debut a fortnight earlier at Flers-Courcelette, north of Combles, when a group of six machines supported a successful British attack. The tanks, all from 'C' Company, each received the name of an up-market alcoholic drink: Chablis, Champagne, Chartreuse, Cognac, Cordon Rouge and Crème de Menthe. The historian of 201st Infantry was among those who remarked on 'these contraptions recently deployed by the British that flatten everything in their path; the "crème de menthe" to their initiates'.

Men of 273rd Infantry receive medals from their past CO, Colonel Jean de Prandières (1859–1942), Caix, 28 September 1916. After serving in the front line since 18 June, the regiment was relieved to escape the trenches around Vermandovillers, where several days of continuous heavy rain had rendered living and fighting conditions untenable. A draft of 350 men from the training battalion of 38th Infantry had just been received, 'mainly youngsters from the class of 1916 and excellent quality'. Colonel de Prandières commanded 273rd Infantry at the start of the offensive in July but had since moved on.

A soldier hunts through the ruins of Deniécourt, 23 September 1916. The village had fallen to the French in one of Foch's small-scale attacks of late September. This man is searching for driving bands to make rings and other souvenirs. The hunt was fraught with peril: 'At coffee time, a loud explosion made us jump', reported Abbé Charles Thellier, a padre serving with a stretcher-bearer unit. 'Shouts of distress. Cries for help. What's up? One of our artillerymen, a great crafter of battlefield souvenirs, has clumsily set off a shell just where I conducted a service two hours ago. Eight of his comrades are wounded, three seriously . . . The stretcher-bearers arrive, and in biting cold, under leaden skies, a desolate cortège of eight litters sets off down the empty road, carrying its groaning burden towards the field hospital, the operating table, the graveyard.'

Men of 109th Infantry operate an optical signalling post, Bois des Satyres, west of Estrées, 21 September 1916. The regiment had entered the line on 7 September: 'the countryside is flat, covered in copses that now contain just a handful of ravaged trees …This is an awful relief, the communication trenches are in a dreadful state, blocked by corpses and all kinds of debris. It's always like this after an action – the relieved unit unable to do anything due to losses and lack of time.'

A soldier grabs a moment to write a letter, Bois des Satyres, west of Estrées, 22 September 1916. The German front line here was 'just a line of individual scrapes', but hampered by heavy rain and mud it had taken the men of 329th Infantry five days to secure Estrées. The villages to the south, Soyécourt and Deniécourt, remained in German hands until the widening of the offensive in September, when they fell after two days' hard fighting by the men of 49th Division.

Advancing from Le Forêt, a heavily laden battalion picks its way through Bois d'Anderlu, 11–13 September 1916. Driving north-eastwards in a notable example of Allied cooperation, the north-bank village of Combles was outflanked – to the east by the French, to the west by the British.

These soldiers have found a billet in the cellars of the Château de Lamotte, Combles, 29 September 1916. 'Combles has fallen,' reported Marcel Sauvage (350th Infantry). 'The men of 110th Infantry and 73rd Infantry have returned: lumps of mud, robotic, ashen, hairy. We ask them nothing and they say nothing. Who knows where their minds wander? They're exhausted: out of strength, nerves shattered, ill, hallucinating. Prisoners troop by in small, sorry groups.'

COMBLES 15.10.16.

The shattered remains of Combles are recorded by an F33 observation crew, 15 October 1916. Beyond is the near-featureless ground towards Sailly-Saillisel. Marcel Sauvage (350th Infantry) described the scene: 'Roads full of potholes crammed with rubble from the houses. Unrelenting guns; a fever deep in the brain. A few artillerymen in the cellars. Wagons destroyed, German graffiti, arrows. Dead horses, bigger than elephants – and bursting open quite horribly. Mules and little donkeys with very gentle expressions. No postmaster. Already the lines are several kilometres further forward. Ravines. Toxic atmosphere: smoke from the explosions, the stench of dead bodies and earth. The Germans dug impregnable shelters, aid posts, round here; now the enemy shells are blowing up the entrances, sealing the reinforced caverns. Some of our troops using them as a refuge are buried alive. Rockets of all shades. We're relieving the front lines.'

A burial party dig graves for their comrades on the battlefield north of Combles, 27 September 1916. French soldiers were buried initially in the Combles Communal Cemetery Extension, but were later transferred to the military cemetery at Rancourt, built in 1921. Rancourt is the largest French military cemetery in the *département* of the Somme, the final resting place of 8,563 men.

German prisoners are hustled down a sunken road, Ravin du Bois Saucisse, west of Cléry-sur-Somme, 25 September 1916. These men are the first to be captured in the attack.

Divisional stretcher-bearers, identifiable from their Red Cross armband, watch as a German prisoner has his documents checked, Ravin du Bois Saucisse, west of Cléry-sur-Somme, 25 September 1916. A month or so later, 296th Infantry captured an enemy officer near Combles. 'Haughty and seething at his bad luck, [he] was taken to the major's dugout', reported Louis Barthas (296th Infantry. 'When the major turned up, the German wouldn't budge. Lieutenant Guillot, CO of 13th Company, was present. "Salute, it's the major," he said in German. Still the Boche refused to move. A second request, the same disdainful response. Lieutenant Guillot slapped him hard on both cheeks. The German turned pale, then red, then saluted, rage in his heart.'

A 120mm battery settles among the former German positions, Ravin de la Pestilence, near Maurepas, 20 September 1916. 'Here we are!' reported René Évrard (162nd Infantry). 'The usual backdrop, ruined buildings, scorched earth, rubbish and debris. One sector of the front looks much like any other. It's been a while since anything surprised us. We're "billeted" in what is clearly an abandoned quarry, with nothing around but a load of loose rock. Two hundred metres away is a ravine they call the "Ravin de la Pestilence", which is out of bounds to us.'

French troops make way for a convoy of Daimler lorries carrying British soldiers towards the front, Maricourt, 7 September 1916. Although described in the official caption as African, the passengers probably belong to the British West Indies Regiment, whose 3rd Battalion served in France as a labour battalion from March 1916. The signboard behind the leading vehicle points the way back to Bray-sur-Somme.

Men of 201st Infantry leave the front line, Ferme de Bronfay, near Maricourt, 23 September 1916. 'How glad we were to receive the orders for our relief on the evening of 16 [September]', recalled the regimental history. 'It was completed under a triple barrage, but no one was hit.' The men were loaded into lorries at Hardécourt-aux-Bois, 'blessed be they that for once were taking us to rest'. The 201st was a pre-war reserve regiment whose depot in Cambrai (Nord) now lay behind the German lines. Consequently, it required drafts from other regiments to keep it up to strength, including a group of forty-five Senegalese troops, as pictured here.

A canal gunboat patrols the Canal de la Somme, near Éclusier, 9 September 1916. After the front line stabilized in late 1914, the French sought to exploit their extensive canal system by constructing eight gunboat barges to offer mobile artillery support to the front line. Lettered A to D and F to I, and each armed with a 14cm gun, the eight vessels formed two batteries. A third battery was composed of four larger barges (K, L, M and O), each armed with two 14cm guns. All three batteries saw service in Belgium, on the Somme and the Oise, and in Champagne. The barges were crewed by naval personnel, who also manned some railway artillery units.

British troops withdraw to rest in French transport, near Suzanne, 1 October 1916. The vehicles are commandeered Paris buses. These men belonged to the Guards Division, which had taken part in the capture of Lesboeufs on 25 September.

The weary men of 363rd Infantry slog their muddy way out of the front line, near Étinehem, 5 September 1916. Over the first three days of September, the regiment had been heavily engaged on the Cléry-Maurepas road, advancing over 1,200m, but at the cost of 21 officers and 615 men.

A group of distinguished visitors examine a 400mm railway gun, Hangest-en-Santerre, 1 September 1916. Favourable publicity in books and newspapers was deemed vital to the war effort, and many writers were given tours of the Front. This group includes (left to right): an anonymous officer; author and politician Joseph Reinach (1856–1921); British author H G Wells (1866–1946), and author Henry Bidou (1873–1943). Their guide is artillery staff officer Jean-Jacques Carence (1871–1953). Wells was quick to highlight the central role of the artillery: 'Now the operations of this modern infantry ... are determined almost completely by the artillery preparation. Artillery is now the most essential instrument of war. You may still get along with rather bad infantry; you may still hold out even after the loss of the aerial ascendancy, but so soon as your guns fail you approach defeat. The backbone process of the whole art of war is the manufacture in overwhelming quantities, the carriage and delivery of shell upon the vulnerable points of the enemy's positions.'

This field ambulance is equipped by motor- and horse-drawn transport, near Frise, September 1916. The motor ambulance was a gift from the French Relief Fund of Great Britain, which donated fifty vehicles to the French army in 1915. For much of the war the charity lay under suspicion of dubious financial practices, although no charges were ever brought.

A Kerr Stuart narrow-gauge locomotive has derailed while hauling a cargo of logs, near Proyart, 20 September 1916. To compensate for losses inflicted by enemy action, the French acquired up to seventy locos manufactured by this firm, based in Stoke-on-Trent.

Chapter Five

The End of the Offensive

The limited Allied offensives of September 1916 – conducted by Sixth Army and Tenth Army for the French, Fourth Army and Reserve Army for the British – were successful only in attritional terms. They wore down the German defenders, but there was always another ridge to take, another village, wood or trench redoubt blocking the advance. Nor was it just the enemy who were facing exhaustion; the attackers too were running short of troops and ammunition.

Throughout October, with intermittent summer downpours turning to persistent heavy rain, Allied commanders from Joffre downwards grew increasingly disillusioned. The larger set-piece attacks were discontinued, to be replaced by small-scale affairs, accompanied by less powerful bombardments and offering ever-diminishing returns in terms of territory gained. On 7 October, Sixth Army mounted an attack north of the Somme on the village of Sailly-Saillisel, seeking to outflank the German positions in Bois Saint-Pierre-Vaast. Fresh troops were brought in for this action – IX Corps (General Horace Pentel) – but could make no progress in fog, wind and rain over the waterlogged, shell-cratered plain. Inserted into the line, XXXII Corps (General Maurice-Eugène Debeney) reached Sailly on 15 October, but it took six more days of house-to-house fighting to eject the bulk of the defenders and another month to kill, capture or drive off every last German.

'IX Corps has done nothing, of course,' wrote Fayolle on 24 October.

> I wonder if it's possible to communicate with the troops there. They can't be digging any trenches or communications trenches, so there's no way of getting forward to lead them. And the artillery! They probably have no observers . . . Certain of their commanders are hopeless. The weather is abysmal.

Fayolle lost patience with Pentel and sacked him two days later, but to no avail. With Sailly in French hands, an outflanking manoeuvre was launched, and when this too failed to make the progress anticipated, Foch ordered a frontal attack. Thigh deep in the quagmire, it was hardly surprising that the infantry could make no ground at all.

South of the river Tenth Army renewed its attacks, making some progress but unable to prise the Germans from the fortified village of Barleux or to penetrate the woods west of Chaulnes. Worse still, a vigorous German counter-attack on 29 October seized the La Maisonnette position, opening a gap in the French lines that fortunately remained unexploited. Staunch German defence, deteriorating weather, and the churned ground all contributed to the stalemate. 'This is the finish of campaigning and the end of the battle of the Somme', concluded Fayolle on 9 November. But next day the indefatigable Foch seemed determined to fight on. 'A winter campaign in these conditions, it's unthinkable', protested Fayolle.

As 1916 drew to a close Joffre was planning further operations for Foch's Northern Army Group, starting on 1 February 1917 – but without any British involvement. 'It is clear that . . . the British . . . will tolerate no further intervention in the conduct of their operations', General des Vallières reported from Haig's HQ in late October. They were, he concluded, likely to stop operations on the Somme and spend the winter 'honing and reinforcing the instrument with which they believe they can play the leading role in the coalition in 1917'. Looking ahead in mid-November, General Fayolle was equally disillusioned with his allies: '[It] seems simple to me: no more joint operations with the British, we don't march in step and we get in each other's way; on our side, open two fronts. First hit one to pull in the reserves; then launch the main effort on the other.'

But French politicians had seen enough. While Foch had delivered success in the opening phases of the offensive, his methodical approach now faced criticism for its inflexibility, for failing to give local commanders sufficient scope to exploit opportunities on the ground. 'We were under pressure to produce a decisive result', recalled Finance Minister Alexandre Ribot. 'Fighting another battle of the Somme, driving back the enemy solely by means of a prolonged series of attacks with short-range objectives, was out of the question.' Joffre was kicked upstairs, named a Marshal of France, the first since the days of Napoleon III, and appointed 'technical adviser' to the government – an empty title for a non-job. Meanwhile Foch had made too many enemies, military and political, to succeed him. Indeed, to save his own skin, Joffre had been quite prepared to sacrifice his senior commander. Foch was recalled to Paris on spurious grounds of 'exhaustion' and effectively sidelined in a series of posts that distanced him from combat command.

The new commander-in-chief, General Robert Nivelle, had come to prominence that autumn at Verdun, gaining lustre in retaking the emblematic strongholds of Fort Vaux and Fort Douaumont and regaining much of the ground lost to the Germans earlier in the year. As commander of Second Army, this former artilleryman had perfected a system that relied on close inter-arms cooperation, the infantry following directly on the heels of an intense rolling barrage. These methods, claimed Nivelle, would be easy to scale up and apply across the front. It was 'the formula' to produce a breakthrough, and the politicians believed him. Fayolle, too, was vilified for his battlefield caution and replaced at the head of Sixth Army by General Charles Mangin, a Nivelle protégé who had also enhanced his reputation at Verdun. 'Cretins!' fumed Fayolle. Of the senior Somme commanders, only Micheler emerged unscathed, transferred from Tenth Army to the command of Reserve Army Group in Nivelle's proposed new offensive.

As a means of relieving pressure on Verdun, the Somme offensive was undoubtedly a success. Over the summer, the diversion of troops and matériel slowed the tempo of German attacks on the Meuse, and in the autumn it was the transfer of units to the Somme that allowed the French counter-attacks at Verdun to succeed. The number of German casualties also had an impact: the class of 1917 was called up in the summer of 1916, eighteen months ahead of time, to be followed in September by the class of 1918; and after spending the winter on construction work, the Germans retreated in March 1917 to the Hindenburg Line, a shorter front behind prepared defences, the better to exploit their reduced numbers.

In terms of a breakthrough, however, the offensive failed. Experience on the Somme and the Meuse seemed to demonstrate the impossibility of piercing the enemy defences to reach open country beyond. By the time the offensive wound down, the French had gained no more than a toehold on the Bapaume–Péronne–Ham road, around Sailly-Saillisel. Tenacious German defence against overwhelming odds, bad weather, churned-up ground, chaos and confusion in the combat zone and the logistical difficulties of sustaining a battle of such length and intensity in a confined area with an inadequate infrastructure all played their part. On 1 July, the opening day of the battle, the French captured much of the German first line, advancing 8km into the enemy positions along an almost 20km front, but resources were lacking to launch the assault crossing of the river and canal needed to make further progress. Nor could the French advance their artillery, particularly the heavier pieces, far enough or fast enough over the battlefield to give the infantry the continuous support so successful at the off, fatally slowing the tempo of attacks. Had the British succeeded in their attacks further north, further French advances may have been possible, but only at the cost of subverting the original operational concept and turning a French attack in support of the British into the main effort.

As a joint operation, too, the Somme offensive left the Allies disenchanted. While their strategy was coherent and their tactics appropriate, French and British armies struggled to coordinate their efforts on any permanent basis, and Foch later bemoaned their inability to find a 'suitable rhythm' to exploit local successes. He also argued that the attacking front was too narrow, that a broader assault would have produced greater profit. Had he remained in post, he would have pressed to renew the offensive in 1917, but on a 100km front extending from Vimy Ridge south to Bapaume, and supported by tanks, additional 155mm guns, and an expanded railway network.

Meanwhile the French had paid a heavy price for their role in the campaign. According to official records, French casualties between 1 July and 20 November amounted to 202,567 killed, wounded, captured or missing, including 49,859 in July, and 76,147 in September, the months of the biggest attacks. To compensate for the losses incurred here and at Verdun, the army was reorganized: the youngest territorial classes were transferred into the 'active' force, while each division was cut from four infantry regiments to three. And morale also suffered. Many soldiers seemed pessimistic about the future, noted reports from postal censorship officials: some men claimed the British were not pulling their weight, others that France had been duped into entering the war. Like André Tanquerel (158th Infantry), killed on 7 November 1916, many just wanted to see an end to the conflict: 'The battle of the Somme is a con', Tanquerel wrote in a letter home.

A trick to part fools and their money . . . That's all. It's easy to be enthusiastic when you don't have to fight. For us, though . . . But what's the point of telling you this? You won't believe me. You'll say I'm just having you on. And that's just what we all find so hard to bear, the thought that our cries of distress are mistaken for peals of laughter.

Clearly, some of the seeds of the 1917 mutinies had already been planted on the Somme.

British and French troops pick through the ruins of Guillemont, 12 December 1916. After falling to the British on 3 September, this village, 3km west of Combles, passed into the French sector three weeks later. British Official Photographer Geoffrey Malins thought it 'an absolute impossibility to tell where the fields ended and the village began'.

A Senegalese working party makes its way down Boyau d'Argonne, a communications trench near the park of the château, Belloy-en-Santerre, October 1916. Each man is carrying a 58mm trench mortar bomb. Although virtually wiped out in the fighting of July and August, Belloy remained a key strongpoint in the French lines south of the river.

Weary men rest at a first-aid post of 1st Zouaves, Bois de Chaulnes, 21 October 1916. The 1st Zouaves Régiment de Marche had formed part of 25th Division since July 1915. After two months of tough fighting south of the Somme, 'on completely churned-up ground made impassable by constant rain', not to mention 'the losses, hardship and fatigue', their transfer to 48th Division in December 1916 was greeted with relief.

General Jean-Baptiste Marchand (1863–1934), commander of 10th Colonial Division, appears with his staff, Piennes (Meurthe-et-Moselle), June 1916. An energetic colonial soldier, Marchand was famed for a dramatic action in 1896, when he force-marched a column from Brazzaville in the French Congo to Fashoda (now Kodok, South Sudan), aiming to halt what the French viewed as British expansionism in Sudan. His resulting confrontation with Sir Herbert Kitchener brought the two countries to the verge of war. Wounded several times during the First World War, he never progressed beyond a divisional command.

Conditions were little better behind the front line. Here, men strain to manoeuvre a long 120mm by muscle-power alone, October 1916. 'The weather is appalling and it's very hard to get hold of fresh supplies of ammunition,' reported Charles Barberon (121st Heavy Artillery). 'We're 500m from a passable road. We can only be reached across fields that are sodden and pitted with shell-holes. Ten or a dozen horses are needed to bring up twenty-five shells. And as we're firing a lot the poor beasts are soon worn out. It's tough on the drivers as well. It might take them twelve hours to complete one trip. The utter exhaustion of the battery (animals and men) is the main reason for our relief, which happened on 16 October.'

A horse-drawn artillery supply wagon makes its muddy way from a depot, west of Maricourt, October 1916. Sergeant Léon Victor Limacher (1894–1986) arrived in the front line with 110th Infantry) in September 1916. He quoted with approval transport engineer Colonel Edmond Lorieux: 'In [his] memory, of all the muds that, for the poilu, inflicted some of the cruellest suffering of the war, first prize went to the mud of the Somme. Heavy, sticky mud, no risk of disappearing as in the Woëvre, but mud you just couldn't get out of!'

Drums and bugles to the fore, a regiment marches out of the line, Bray-sur-Somme, 11 October 1916. Despite a few complaints about the facilities in Amiens, Charles Barberon (121st Heavy Artillery) still relished his short period of leave: 'the food is mediocre, the sleeping accommodation poor and the table as sparse as at the front. We don't lack for entertainment, or cash when we arrive, so each man tries to spend up as quickly as possible. When the future is so uncertain, the soldier looks for immediate pleasures of any kind. He throws all caution to the winds: who knows what tomorrow may bring. Let's enjoy today. His usual hardships make him even keener on having a good time.'

The mobile cookers belch forth steam at the cookhouse of a battalion of *chasseurs alpins*, near Hardécourt-aux-Bois, 22 October 1916. Cheese is clearly on the menu! The Emmental seen here was initially the preferred ration cheese. Although robust, easily transportable and a good keeper, each 85–110kg wheel required 1,000l of milk and supplies began to run short. Camembert used half this amount of milk per kilo of cheese, and its producers stepped into the breach. Pre-war sales of Camembert were restricted to its native Normandy, to Paris and the larger towns of northern France, but its issue to the army created the national market it still enjoys today.

Transport drivers arrive at a well-stocked military co-operative, Moreuil, 18 November 1916. The men are clad in a variety of scarves and goatskin coats to ward off the cold. Selling foodstuffs to supplement the official rations, co-operatives had been set up by a number of regiments and formations to shield their men from profiteers and high prices in the rear. In late 1916 it was ordered that one should be established in every division.

The 145mm naval gun *Caroline* fires, Hardécourt-aux-Bois, 22 October 1916. This pattern was deployed in small numbers on the Western Front in 1916. It reused the barrels from two old battleships, *Carnot* and *Charles Martel*, fitted with new recuperating systems plus a new mount and trail.

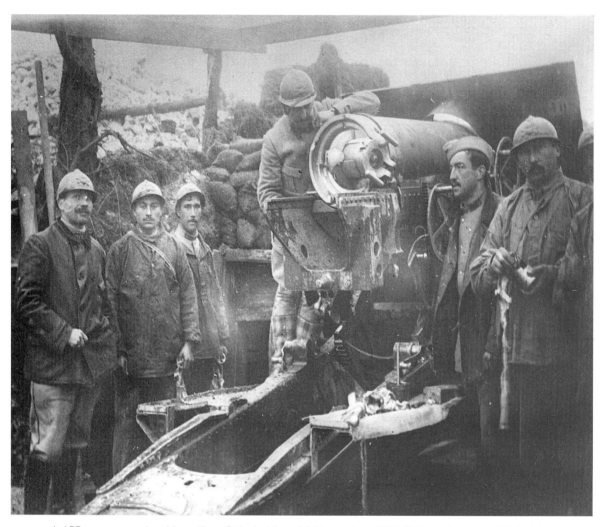

A 155mm gun equips this artillery, Bois de Hem, 20 November 1916. This particular model features the reused barrel of an obsolete 1877-pattern Bange 155L, fitted to a new carriage. The modifications allowed a more powerful charge to be used, adding 900m to the gun's range and putting it out of reach of most German artillery. 'The gunners are happy,' reported Jean-Marie Bonnery (81st Infantry). 'We're going to rest in a spot previously occupied by our 155s.'

A French artillery convoy passes a Highland battalion, near Ferme de Bronfay, between Maricourt and Bray, 6 December 1916. Louis Barthas (296th Infantry) described the encampment at Ferme de Bronfay: 'No symmetry, not many barrack huts erected yet, but a whole variety of shelters in canvas, or made from planks, broken crates, branches and tree trunks. Some British officers have smart huts with all the creature comforts. Thousands of British recruits have learned the noble profession of arms at this camp, which covers several hundred hectares. It's a veritable human anthill, criss-crossed by roads filled night and day with endless convoys of cars, trucks, heavy caissons, vehicles of all kinds, relief columns, ambulances etc.'

Heading for the crossing at Cappy, a convoy of Berliet lorries travels along Rue Neuve, Suzanne, 6 December 1916. Marius Berliet was a pioneer of the French motor industry, designing his first lorry in 1906. By 1916, his factory just outside Lyon (Rhône) was turning out forty CBA trucks a day for the French war effort, supplying the Verdun and Somme fronts.

French soldiers and Royal Engineers enjoy a little roadside *entente cordiale*, near Guillemont, 6 December 1916. Many Frenchmen were curious about their allies, among them Georges Duhamel (Ambulance 9/3): 'There were some shared roads where the French and British were neighbours. That's where we saw the fine British artillery, brand new – gleaming, no patina of age – draped in pale tack with tin-plate buckles, horses picked for their coats, thick and glossy like circus mounts. The infantry also marched past: all young men. A variety of pipes and drums played a wild African-sounding music. And then big racked-out vans came bumping along, evacuating the wounded, fair hair, dazed expressions, as placid as travellers with Thomas Cook's.'

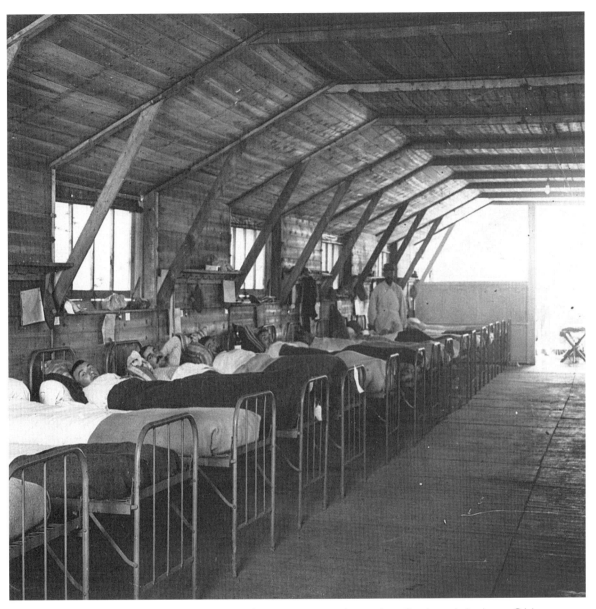

A lines of communication hospital experiences some respite as the offensive winds down, Cérisy-Gailly, 17 November 1916. Alphonse Pasquier, a local resident, had witnessed the hospital in action during the battle: 'the huts were full, the wounded placed wherever space could be found, on a stretcher, even just a blanket. The surgeons performed amputations; the stretcher-bearers and nurses bustled around. As soon as they'd been bandaged, those with light wounds were loaded into the hospital train that left every day for warmer climes.'

An F33 observation flight records the impact of a German air raid on a heavy artillery ammunition depot, Cérisy-Gailly, 10 November 1916. The enemy raid had taken place on the night of 6–7 November, when a bomb hit an incoming munitions train, with the flames reportedly visible in Amiens, 25km away. Although the station building was destroyed, and roofs and windows were damaged for miles around, no one was killed. Still, local civilians thought it prudent to take to their cellars for next few nights in case the raiders returned.

The hospital barge *Ville d'Arras* proceeds along the Canal de la Somme, near Cérisy-Gailly, November 1916. The wounded were also evacuated by barge, transferring them from the lines of communication hospitals at Cérisy-Gailly and Bray-sur-Somme for further treatment at base hospitals in Amiens. Although slow, travelling at speeds of 5–10kph, barges offered a very smooth ride, a boon particularly to men with abdominal wounds.

Uniforms and bedding await disinfection at a lines of communications hospital, Cayeux-en-Santerre, 4 December 1916. Each hospital had a sterilization and drying unit consisting of two vehicles – one capable of washing a 300kg load, the other with drying machines. Attached to 1 Colonial Corps, Ambulance 3/3 was in reserve in Pisseleu-aux-Bois (Oise): 'Big crowds have been mobbing our doors since the day we opened', reported Raphaël Weill. 'Tirailleurs africains, chasseurs d'Afrique, gunners, infantrymen, Malagasies – all strip, shower, get dressed again and go for a rub [with a sulphur ointment to treat scabies], while we disinfect their uniforms and delouse their underwear. It's a success!'

A new bridge is needed over the Canal de la Somme, Éclusier, 2 December 1916. The winding multiple channels of the Somme and its neighbouring canal hampered north–south communication in the area at the best of times, so repairing existing bridges and building new ones was a priority.

A navy diver dons his gear, Canal de la Somme, near Frise, 5 October 1916. The diver is helping to repair lock gates destroyed by German explosives earlier in the action. After the offensive closed in late 1916, a huge effort was required to make good the infrastructure of the recently captured territory and to consolidate the new front lines. By November 1918, over half the surface area of the *département* of the Somme (616,329 hectares) required some kind of restoration, including 28,000 hectares in the designated red zone bounded by Albert, Combles, Bray and Péronne. 'I can't see how you could hope to cultivate the land again in these places', concluded adviser Henri Hitier.

Engineers in a petrol-fuelled car inspect a newly built railway line, near Maricourt, 4 November 1916. Situated midway between Albert and Péronne, Maricourt became a useful depot north of the Somme, especially after the German withdrawal to the Hindenburg Line in early 1917.

A steamroller makes good the Morcourt road, near Proyart, 20 October 1916. Morcourt lay en route to the Somme crossing and railway sidings at Cérisy. The smaller roads branching off the main Amiens–Proyart–Belloy route were broken up by the constant weight of traffic. In February Foch had planned for three steamrollers to keep the roads in a good state of repair. By November Northern Army Group had at its disposal forty-nine steam- and petrol-driven rollers, thirty-four mechanical diggers, 8,340 French labourers (mainly from Territorial regiments) and 1,450 prisoners of war. Together they moved 671,000 tonnes of aggregate, not only repairing roads but also building twenty-three new roads into the battle zone.

Péronne is left a wreck after the Germans withdraw to the Hindenburg Line, March 1917. 'Don't rage, just marvel', reads the sign now conserved in the town's Historial de la Grande Guerre. 'Péronne, which used to be a lovely little town on the Somme, is nothing but a huge mound of rubble', lamented Gunner Ernst Pauleit (Feld-Artillerie-Regiment Nr. 7) from his observation post in the attic of a ruined house. 'Not a house in this town of some 5,000 peacetime inhabitants is undamaged ... All in all a bleak prospect when the once-happy residents return. Repairing the damage is inconceivable. The only way to revive these ruins will be to demolish and rebuild every home.'

French delegates arrive to confer with their British allies, Boulogne (Pas-de-Calais), October 1916. Their main achievement was to agree reinforcements for the Salonika front. Left to right are the leading French delegates: Navy Minister, Admiral Lucien Lacaze (1860–1955); Finance Minister, Alexandre Ribot (1842–1923); Minister of War, General Pierre Roques (1856–1920); Prime Minister, Aristide Briand (1862–1932); General Joffre; diplomat and civil servant, Pierre de Margerie (1861–1942); Under-Secretary of State, Albert Thomas (1878–1932); and Minister of State, Léon Bourgeois (1851–1925). Among the British delegates were the Prime Minister, Herbert Asquith; Foreign Secretary, Viscount Grey; Secretary for War, David Lloyd George; First Lord of the Admiralty, Arthur Balfour; and Chief of the Imperial General Staff, General Sir William Robertson.

The French top brass attend a firepower demonstration, Bayon (Meurthe-et-Moselle), 20 November 1916. Left to right are: General Joffre; President Poincaré, General Louis Franchet d'Espèrey (1856–1942), commander of Eastern Army Group; General Alexis Hély d'Oisel (1859–1937), commander of VIII Corps; and Colonel Ambroise Desprès (1868–1944), French military attaché in Romania. For Joffre, two years of failed attempts to drive the Germans from French soil would soon come home to roost. Within a month he was sacked and replaced as commander-in-chief by General Robert Nivelle.

General Foch entertains leading Radical politician Georges Clemenceau (1841–1929), Northern Army Group HQ, Villers-Bretonneux, 9 October 1916. Foch was not above playing politics, and may well have had a part in Joffre's downfall, but he too became a victim of the purge of French commanders and was sacked by telegram over the night of 15/16 December. After the pugnacious Clemenceau was appointed prime minister in 1918, Foch would return as Allied Supreme Commander and prove himself a determined coalition leader.

General Robert Nivelle (centre) arrives in newly liberated Noyon (Oise), 24 March 1917. The new commander-in-chief has eyes only for the camera as a civic dignitary offers his greetings. Fresh from recent victory in command of Second Army at Verdun, the bullish Nivelle was Joffre's preferred candidate as his successor. Nivelle claimed to 'have the formula' to defeat the Germans and, unlike Foch, promised a rapid route to victory. 'The experiment is conclusive', he told the men of his old command on his departure for GQG. 'Our method has shown its effectiveness. Victory is certain, I guarantee. As the enemy will learn to his cost.'